# HIRAM JOHNSON

**Recent Titles in**
**Bio-Bibliographies in Law and Political Science**

Wayne Morse: A Bio-Bibliography
*Lee Wilkins*

Will Herberg: A Bio-Bibliography
*Harry J. Ausmus*

# HIRAM JOHNSON

## A Bio-Bibliography

## Michael A. Weatherson
### and
### Hal Bochin

Bio-Bibliographies in Law and Political Science, Number 3

**Greenwood Press**
New York • Westport, Connecticut • London

**Library of Congress Cataloging-in-Publication Data**

Weatherson, Michael A., 1952-
  Hiram Johnson : a bio-bibliography.

  (Bio-bibliographies in law and political science,
ISSN 0882-7052 ; no. 3)
  Bibliography: p.
  Includes index.
  1. Johnson, Hiram, 1866-1945—Bibliography.
2. Johnson, Hiram, 1866-1945. 3. Legislators—United
States—Biography. 4. United States. Congress.
Senate—Biography. I. Bochin, Hal. II. Title.
III. Series.
E748.J73W43  1988      973.91'092'4 [B]  87-28030
ISBN 0-313-25574-1 (lib. bdg. : alk. paper)

British Library Cataloguing in Publication Data is available.

Library of Congress Catalog Card Number: 87-28030
ISBN: 0-313-25574-1
ISSN: 0882-7052

First published in 1988

Greenwood Press, Inc.
88 Post Road West, Westport, Connecticut 06881

Printed in the United States of America

The paper used in this book complies with the
Permanent Paper Standard issued by the National
Information Standards Organization (Z39.48-1984).

10 9 8 7 6 5 4 3 2 1

**Copyright Acknowledgment**

The authors and publisher would like to gratefully acknowledge
permission to use the following:

Hiram W. Johnson Papers (C-B 581), The Bancroft Library,
University of California, Berkeley.

# Contents

# Preface

Senator Hiram W. Johnson (1866-1945) of California held
a position of leadership in the progressive movement and for
more than thirty-five years influenced America's foreign and
domestic policies. Best remembered for his role in the birth
of the National Progressive Party and as Theodore Roosevelt's
running-mate in the 1912 presidential election, Johnson
advocated economic and social reform. As governor of
California he led the nation in putting progressive ideas
into practice. As a United States senator, he gained a
national platform and presidential consideration. A
unilateralist in foreign policy, Johnson provided significant
opposition to American involvement in the League of Nations,
the World Court, and even the United Nations. In dealing
with other nations, every president from Woodrow Wilson to
Franklin Roosevelt had to take into account the position of
Hiram Johnson.

Although other leaders of the progressive movement have
attracted considerable attention from scholars, Johnson has
been ignored for the most part. No biographies of Johnson
have been published thus far, and he has neither been given
much credit for his contributions nor been given a proper
place within the context of American history. Undoubtedly,
his unique role in the progressive movement, as well as his
influence on foreign policy, deserve more consideration.

This work is directed toward scholars interested in the
growth and decline of progressivism and in the development of
American foreign policy between 1910 and 1945. As a bio-
bibliography of Johnson, the book is divided into two major
sections. It begins with a biographical sketch of Johnson's
political career, thus providing a perspective on
California's progressive era, the League of Nations
controversy, the Great Depression and the New Deal, the
controversy over the reorganization of the Supreme Court, and
preparation for World War II. Quotations from his major

speeches, newspaper accounts of his campaigns, and excerpts from personal letters are included.

The biographical sketch is followed by an annotated bibliography that is divided into a collection of selected works mentioning Johnson, articles written by Johnson, a collection of important speeches taken from the Congressional Record, and an appendix of manuscript collections of unpublished correspondence. The first segment of the bibliography includes citations of major historical and contemporary materials about Johnson. In some cases the authors have provided their own judgments as to the value and accuracy of this material. In addition, a list is included of major newspapers where accounts of Johnson's campaign speaking can be found. The second segment provides an annotated listing of significant periodical articles written by Johnson, important Senate reports he authored, and edited collections of his personal letters. A third segment offers summaries of more than one hundred of Johnson's most representative Senate and radio addresses, documenting Johnson's opinion on every significant issue facing the country. Quotations from the speeches are offered to illustrate the flavor of Johnson's remarks.

The numbers in parentheses in the biographical sketch refer to the primary and secondary sources annotated in the second part of the book. The numbered, annotated materials provide complete citations and generally refer to specific pages within the text. In the index the numbers in parentheses refer to the numbered annotations and the other numbers refer to pages in the biographical sketch.

Given the length of Johnson's public career and the great number of historical sources available, the authors have selected for annotation those contemporaneous materials that provide significant information about Johnson's personal or public life and those scholarly analyses that offer the most insight. The authors hope these reference materials together with the biographical sketch and Johnson's own words in letters, speeches, and articles will contribute to a greater appreciation of Johnson's role in the progressive movement and in the shaping of American foreign policy.

# Acknowledgments

This book would not have been possible without institutional support and the personal help of several individuals to whom we owe a special debt of gratitude.

In particular, we would like to express our appreciation to California State University, Fresno, for an assigned time research grant and the staffs of the special collections and government publications departments at the Henry Madden Library for their invaluable assistance in locating materials. We also wish to express our appreciation to James D. Hart of the Bancroft Library, University of California, Berkeley, for permission to quote from the Hiram W. Johnson Papers, an invaluable resource.

We thank Thomas B. Harte, a friend and colleague, for his time and criticism, Ray Ewing for his support, and Carlos Aleman for his research assistance. A special thanks is given to Mildred Vasan whose editorial pen improved the readability of our drafts immeasurably.

# Chronology

| | |
|---|---|
| 1866 | September 2, born to Grove and Ann Johnson in Sacramento, California. |
| 1878 | Recites "Sheridan's Last Ride" for President Grant during his visit to California. |
| 1884 | Enters the freshman class at the University of California, Berkeley; joins baseball team and Chi Phi fraternity; chosen class orator. |
| 1886 | Leaves college in his junior year in order to wed Minnie McNeal, daughter of a successful Sacramento contractor; goes to work in his father's law office as a stenographer. |
| 1888 | Passes bar exam and becomes a law partner with his father and brother, Albert. |
| 1893 | Presents a Memorial Day address to the local townspeople. |
| 1894 | Successfully manages his father's campaign for Republican representative in the 54th Congress. |
| 1896 | Hiram and his brother end their partnership with their father as a result of political differences with him. |
| 1900 | Defends George H. Clark when his election as mayor is contested on a technicality by local political bosses; successfully takes his case through the state supreme court. |
| 1901 | Publishes his own small paper, The Independent. |
| 1902 | Johnson and his brother move their law office to San |

Francisco.

1906    His home and office are destroyed in the San
        Francisco earthquake.

1907    Appointed assistant prosecutor in the San Francisco
        graft trials.

1908    Replaces Francis Heney as chief prosecutor in the
        Abraham Ruef case; presents a scathing denunciation
        of Ruef, the major political boss charged with graft
        and bribery; Ruef is convicted.

1909    Joins the Lincoln-Roosevelt League and gives several
        speeches supporting political reform.

1910    Nominated by the Lincoln-Roosevelt League as their
        candidate for governor; conducts the first stump
        campaign for governor in the state's history; wins
        the Republican primary and the general election.

1911    Successfully conducts a stump campaign to gain
        support for amendments to the state constitution
        which included the initiative, referendum, and
        recall of elected officials.

1912    Represents California as a delegate to National
        Republican Convention in Chicago; walks out
        protesting the convention proceedings; calls for the
        formation of a new party; accepts the vice-
        presidential nomination at the first National
        Progressive Party Convention.

1913    Meets with Secretary of State William Jennings
        Bryan, representing President Woodrow Wilson, over
        the proposed anti-alien legislation in California.
        Pressured by overwhelming popular support and a near
        unanimous vote by the state legislature, Johnson
        signs the anti-alien bill into law.

1914    Becomes the first governor of California to be
        reelected to a second term.

1916    Returns to the Republican party, vowing his support
        for Charles Evans Hughes; is elected senator by a
        wide margin, while Hughes is narrowly defeated in
        California.

1917    Resigns as governor and presents his farewell
        address to the California legislature; his first
        vote in the U.S. Senate is for a declaration of war
        against Germany.

1919    Attacks Wilson on his decision to represent U.S. at
        treaty negotiations; joins with 37 other senators

declaring their opposition to the Versailles Treaty in its current form; presents a major address on June 2, outlining his opposition to the treaty and the League of Nations; follows the president during his "Western Tour," refuting Wilson's arguments.

1920    Embarks on a nationwide stump campaign for the presidency; is denied the the nomination at the convention by party bosses despite his success in the primaries; is offered the vice-presidential spot by four different candidates.

1921    Representing the coal miners in West Virginia, successfully sponsors a resolution demanding an investigation of the coal mines.

1921-28    Cosponsors Boulder Canyon bill (Hoover Dam) with Congressman Philip Swing; issue becomes a major campaign promise in 1922 senatorial race.

1922    Runs a successful stump campaign for reelection to the Senate.  Votes for Nine Powers Pact.

1923    Begins his opposition against U.S. entry into the World Court.

1924    Embarks on a nationwide stump campaign, but loses primaries in Illinois, Nebraska, Michigan, and North Dakota; announces his withdrawal from the race on the eve of his loss in California, the only election he ever lost in his home state.

1925    Voices his opposition to the Paris Peace Conference.

1926    Successfully attaches a reservation to World Court resolution forbidding the court from entertaining any request for a decision on a question of interest to the United States without its consent.

1928    Wins another senatorial race; Boulder Dam project is finally approved by Congress.

1929    Votes for Kellogg-Briand Anti-War Treaty, but claims it is of no consequence.

1931    Opposes Hoover's proposal for a moratorium on war debts; rejects request from supporters to become a candidate for the Republican presidential nomination in 1932.

1932    Pledges his support to FDR and embarks on a speaking tour on behalf of the Democratic candidate; turns down offer by FDR to become the secretary of the interior.

1933    Supports Roosevelt's New Deal measures.

1934    Johnson Act, which prevents the president from declaring token payments by European countries as sufficient to meet their war debt obligations, is passed by Congress; reelected to a fourth term in the Senate.

1935    Successfully opposes FDR in his attempt to gain Senate approval of U.S. involvement in the World Court.

1936    Stricken by a cerebral vascular stroke, is unable to participate in the presidential campaign.

1937    Opposes Roosevelt on every major issue; leads opposition against FDR's court packing plan.

1938    Sponsors resolution of inquiry into foreign policy agreements with Great Britain.

1939    Leads opposition against a proposed French purchase of planes and Pittman's "cash and carry" plan.

1940    Reelected to a fifth term in the Senate; endorses Wendell Willkie for president; presents a radio address opposing a third term for FDR.

1941    In a national radio address voices his opposition to lend-lease; votes for a declaration of war against Japan and Germany following the attack on Pearl Harbor.

1943    A stroke paralyzes him for several weeks, limiting his congressional activities to afternoon sessions.

1945    Becomes the sole senator in the Committee on Foreign Relations to vote against the creation of the United Nations; on the same day that the atomic bomb is dropped, August 6, 1945, Johnson dies of a cerebral thrombosis.

# 1

# Biographical Sketch

## Introduction

Hiram Warren Johnson had two distinct political careers. From 1911 to 1917, as the progressive governor of California, he put the people back into government through the adoption of the initiative and referendum processes and supported legislation that improved working conditions for women and children. From 1917 until his death in 1945, he served in the United States Senate where his greatest impact was felt in foreign affairs. His speeches helped kill the League of Nations treaty and prevented American entry into the World Court. He led the opposition to Roosevelt's attempt to aid the allies by circumventing the neutrality laws. As both governor and senator, Johnson defended his beliefs tenaciously, and with the fervor of a revivalist he strove to convert others to his position.

The first governor of California to be reelected for a second term, Johnson turned progressive ideals into law. He eliminated the influence of the Southern Pacific Railroad from the state's politics and successfully promoted major political reform. Such activity soon attracted a national audience. At the 1912 Republican convention, Johnson protested the rejection of delegates representing Theodore Roosevelt and, subsequently, presided at the birth of the Progressive party. Selected as the new party's first vice presidential candidate, Johnson's popularity among the faithful was second only to Roosevelt's. With Woodrow Wilson's victory over both Roosevelt and Taft in the presidential election, Johnson returned to Sacramento where he continued to work for progressive causes.

In 1916 Johnson was elected to the United States Senate where he remained for the next twenty-nine years. Exhibiting little interest in or impact on progressive legislation, he is best remembered for his opposition to the League of Nations and to the World Court. His speeches on foreign policy dramatized the differences between the opposing ideologies of internationalism and noninterventionism. Johnson, more than anyone else, was the primary spokesman for neutrality during the period between World War I and World War II.

A unilateralist, Johnson consistently argued that the United States should not be the "policeman of the world," and he supported the concept of self-determination, arguing that neither the United States nor any other nation had the right to interfere in the internal affairs of another country. Unwilling to trust America's fate to negotiated agreements, he argued for a policy of unilateralism, insisting that actions should be based on self-interest rather than on collective interests. "I am an American" was Johnson's repeated cry.(249)

Due to his position on foreign policy, Johnson was labelled an isolationist by his opponents and by the press. He remained steadfast in his beliefs, however, even in the face of unfavorable public opinion. His views regarding foreign policy often cost him friends and supporters; his stand against the League of Nations in 1920, for example, contributed to his failure to win the Republican presidential nomination that year. Whether in the majority, as in the World Court controversy, or a member of a small minority, as in his opposition to the United Nations, Johnson never wavered.

Described by one of his contemporaries as a "political revivalist,"(24) Johnson invariably viewed himself as a crusader against corruption and injustice and as the last remaining bastion protecting the public from the false prophets of big business. His attack against such interests was a recurring theme in all of his speeches, even in his foreign policy addresses, where he argued that the real villains were the international bankers, who were "picking the pockets" of the American public to support their foreign intrigues.(91) His speeches, like other progressive rhetoric of the period, were based upon the belief that a conspiracy of special interests controlled the government.

Despite the efforts of Johnson and others, the Progressives failed to wrest control of the Republican party from the conservative faction. As a result, Johnson and his colleagues remained a minority force in the political process. Recognizing their inability to determine policy, surviving Progressives, such as Johnson, took pride in their roles as antagonists to the old guard, arguing vehemently against those policies with which they disagreed. Johnson, for example, always perceived himself as a man of high integrity fighting for what he believed was right and in the best interest of the nation. While campaigning during the 1922 senatorial election, Johnson defended his unpopular vote against the Four Power Pact by emphasizing:

I conceive the duty of a public official to give all that
is in him to those he represents.  He can do this only
with his best judgment and following his conscience.   If
he is the mere weather vane of transient public clamor,
he merits no man's respect, and worse still,  he loses
his own. . . .  I never was and I never will be a
mere rubber stamp to register the will of any man or any
set of men.(18)

Throughout his public life, Hiram Johnson fought determinedly
for those goals he thought in the public interest.

## The Roots of Insurgency: Johnson's Early Career

Hiram Johnson never tired of reminding his colleagues
that he had been born and raised in California "which I love
as I love no other place on the face of the earth."(312)
Johnson frankly admitted the selfishness and even
provincialism which often led him to present his views as a
"Californian."  Whether fighting for tariffs to protect
California's agricultural products, or for the water needed
for irrigation and electric power, Johnson eagerly supported
the rapid growth of his native state.

Born September 2, 1866, at the base of the mother lode
of the High Sierras in Sacramento, the state capital of
California, Hiram Warren Johnson was the fourth child of
five, with three sisters and one brother.  His father, Grove
Johnson, was a moderately successful middle class lawyer who
migrated from New York to the West in 1863.  A very ambitious
person, Grove took advantage of any available career
opportunity.  Not only did he practice law but also he sold
insurance and participated actively in local politics.  He
was swampland clerk of Sacramento county from 1866 to 1879
and in 1867 was nominated by the Regular Union party for the
office of county auditor.  He served on the Democratic State
Central Committee and unsuccessfully ran for the state senate
in 1871 and 1875.  Illegal campaign practices (the stuffing
of ballot boxes and the use of invisible ink on ballots to
eliminate his opponent's name) in these elections, however,
disqualified him from office.(21)

Following his third election defeat, Grove Johnson
converted to the Republican party, a move that proved to be
rewarding.  He won election to the California assembly in
1878 and 1879 and to the state senate in 1880.  Later Grove
won a term in the U.S. House of Representatives (54th
Congress, March 1895 to March 1897), and served as a delegate
to the Republican National Convention at St. Louis in 1896.
After losing his seat in the U.S. Congress, he ran
successfully for the state assembly in 1901 and again, after
two more defeats, he won another term in 1907.(18)  Because
of his father's political interests Hiram had an insider's
view of political life.   From his mother Hiram learned to

care for the underdog. Ann Williamson de Montfredy, who traced her ancestry to a general in the Revolutionary War, had married Grove in 1861. She was well educated and considered by those who knew her as a kind and compassionate person. Her influence on Hiram was evident in his nonviolent tendencies, as well as in his deep concern for the conditions of the poor.(1)

Hiram's first public speaking experience occurred in 1878, when at the age of twelve, he recited a poem during General Grant's visit to Sacramento. Selected by his teachers for his ability to recite literature from memory, the young Johnson left a vivid impression on the former president, who according to a local newspaper, "displayed much difficulty in suppressing his emotion during the young Hiram Johnson's spirited recital of 'Sheridan's Last Ride.'"(126)

During his high school years Hiram was frequently asked to recite various passages of poetry. To Johnson the heroic works of Macaulay, Scott, Tennyson, Whittier, and Longfellow were particularly appealing. His son recalled that his father "could recite large portions of Marion and other lengthy poems such as Macaulay's 'Ivry,' 'the Battle of Naseby,' 'Horatius at the Bridge,' 'The Charge of the Light Brigade,' and others of that character." At graduation he served as valedictorian. The speech was fairly ordinary, but after reaching the end of his manuscript Hiram continued with some "extemporaneous remarks on the duties and obligations of young people entering the mature life."(1)

Hiram also demonstrated athletic ability. He loved to swim and in grammar school was pitcher and captain of the school's baseball team. After his uncle, whose name he carried, moved to Sacramento and purchased a small ranch, Hiram spent quite a bit of time playing there. Learning to hunt and fish, he was known later in life as a crack shot with a gun.(1)

Sacramento was still a rough brawling town where attitudes from the gold rush days persisted for a good many years. There were over 111 saloons in the area, and every Saturday night miners came down from the hills for entertainment. The city was controlled by the owners of saloons and gambling houses. One such owner was Frank Rhoades, a notorious Sacramento political boss. It was against such bosses that Grove crusaded. Lincoln Steffens provides an exciting account of a confrontation between Rhoades and the Johnsons:

> The boss of Sacramento, Frank Rhoades, the gambler, was having one of his conventions of the local ring leaders in a room under his gambling house. It was at night. There were no outsiders present, none wanted, and the insiders were fighting, shooting men. During the meeting

Grove L. Johnson, a well-known attorney in the town, walked in with his two sons, Albert and Hiram, both little more than boys, and both carrying revolvers. They went up to the front, and with one of his boys on one side of him, the other on the other, Mr. Johnson told those crooks all about themselves and what they were doing. He was bitter, fearless, free-spoken; he insulted, he defied those politicians; he called upon the town to clean them out and predicted that their power would be broken some day. When he had finished, he and his sons walked out.(18)

Although Grove's prediction was accurate, it took a few more years before the reform movement succeeded in diminishing Rhoades's power. During this period, Hiram and his brother participated in several of Grove's campaigns, speaking on his behalf and canvassing the district for him. When not campaigning, Hiram worked as a stenographer in his father's law office.(21)

In 1884, in keeping with his parent's wishes, Hiram entered the freshman class at the University of California, Berkeley. He immediately joined the Chi Phi fraternity and as a student did well and was prominent in many college activities. During his first and second years he was chosen class orator and he played on the baseball team. Hiram also belonged to the Durant Rhetorical Society and participated in several debates. His aggressiveness earned him the reputation of a leader. As one student remarked, "A freshman is boss of the whole university."(18)

Unfortunately, Hiram never finished his junior year even though he was chosen editor of the Blue and Gold, the university yearbook. He left school to marry Minnie McNeal, the daughter of a successful Sacramento contractor. Stories circulated by family members purported that he married Minnie to prevent her from traveling to Europe to study music. More likely, the pretext of studying music in Europe was only a cover to hide the fact that Minnie was pregnant at the time Hiram married her. The birth of Hiram, Jr. on August 10, 1887, only six and a half months after their marriage, was followed a few years later by the birth of Archibald, their youngest son.(10)

As a wedding gift his father-in-law built a small house in Sacramento for Johnson and his wife. Hiram went back to work as a stenographer in his father's office, studying law whenever possible. Two years later, in 1888, he passed the bar exam and entered the firm as a partner with his father and brother.(21) Because the dramatic phase of planning strategy of argument and counteracting testimony with other testimony greatly appealed to Hiram, he concentrated upon trial cases. His brother, Albert, on the other hand, preferred research and provided his younger brother and father with excellent trial briefs.(1) As a result, the firm prospered.

In 1894 Hiram and his brother managed their father's
first successful campaign for Congress.   Two years later
Grove was renominated by the Republican party to run for
reelection, but, because of his support of the infamous
Powers Funding Bill (a proposal which would have extended the
Southern Pacific's debt to the government for eighty-five
years at extremely low interest rates), his sons advised him
against running on the grounds that his lack of faith with
the people of California and his support of the Southern
Pacific Railroad made his defeat inevitable.(21)   The press
castigated Grove, depicting him as a criminal and traitor.
Although agreeing with the press, Hiram voted for Grove while
participating as a delegate to the Republican county and
district convention.   Nevertheless, he refused to take an
active part in the campaign, and ill-feelings between him and
his father caused him to leave the family law firm.   After
the election Grove moved his law practice to San Francisco;
his sons continued practicing separately in Sacramento.(1)

Johnson was a popular figure in the community.   On
holidays he was often asked to speak.   On Memorial Day in
1893 Johnson delivered an address which gained the praise of
the local press.(18)   During the speech he reminded his
audience that many in the country were so poor that they were
no better off than serfs.  Thus, Johnson used the opportunity
to warn against the concentration of wealth and to argue for
reform.   The speech was so well received that the Sacramento
Record-Union, a major newspaper in the city, reprinted large
portions of the address the following day.   The Sacramento
Bee described Johnson as "the well-known and brilliant young
lawyer of this city," who delivered an "excellent" Memorial
Day oration.(21)

Johnson achieved a significant degree of popularity
through his holiday orations and his success as a local
attorney.   Many believed that he could be elected to any
local office and tried to persuade him to run.   But Johnson
steadfastly refused, preferring to support others.   One such
candidate was George H. Clark, a local mortician, who was
elected mayor of Sacramento in 1900.   When Clark broke with
party leaders and promised to clean out vice and corruption,
the so called "bosses" contested his election on a
technicality.   Outraged by their actions, Hiram "proclaimed
at a stormy meeting of the city's board of trustees that 'he
will remain mayor.'"(21)   Clark remained in office, but only
after Johnson successfully took the case through the state
supreme court.

The political bosses were not intimidated easily.   In
1901 when Clark began his reelection campaign, they refused
to renominate him as the Republican candidate.   Hiram and his
brother, Albert, obtained Clark's nomination by petition as
an Independent.   The local newspapers reacted to political

pressure, however, and united against Clark; and the bosses rented every hall in the city to prevent any reform meetings. In response Johnson and his brother published their own small paper, called the Independent, which they delivered twice a week to every resident in the city. Consisting of only four sheets no larger than half the size of a standard sheet of newsprint, it could hardly be called a newspaper.   Hiram wrote the paper himself, filling it with a barrage of attacks against the local press, William Land (the opposing candidate) and the local political bosses.   Refused meeting halls, Johnson rented a medium-size circus tent and set it up in a different vacant lot every two or three days.(1)    The first tent campaign ever run in the area, it attracted large audiences.

The campaign gained so much support that the party bosses persuaded Grove to return to Sacramento and to campaign against his sons.   On one occasion Grove referred to his sons as, "one Albert, full of booze, and one Hiram, full of egotism."(18)    But, despite Grove's efforts, Clark was reelected, giving the Johnson brothers notoriety beyond the Sacramento area for their successful campaign.   As a reward for his efforts Hiram was appointed the city's corporation counsel at $75 a month.(18)

In 1902 Hiram and his brother joined forces and moved to San Francisco to open a law office in the larger city.   With Albert's research skills and Hiram's courtroom tactics they rarely lost a case.   Unfortunately, the partnership was short-lived.   Inflicted with alcoholism, Albert began having difficulties fulfilling his duties.   Sometimes he disappeared for days leaving Hiram without help in the office.   By 1905 Albert's problem became so acute that Hiram left the partnership to open his own law firm.(1)   Practicing alone, Johnson had no difficulty attracting clients and was considered one of the best lawyers in the city.    His practice, however, was disrupted by the 1906 earthquake when Johnson lost his home and office during the fire that followed.

Like so many other cities in the country, San Francisco was deeply controlled by bossism; vice, corruption, and bribery were rampant.   The city was in the grip of corrupt officials, and for years reformers, like Fremont Older of the San Francisco Bulletin, fought unsuccessfully to rid the city of them.    The 1906 earthquake and fire, however, finally created the atmosphere for reform.   Supported by President Roosevelt, they enlisted the services of William J. Burns--later to open the famous detective agency--and the cooperation of William H. Langdon, the district attorney. Francis J. Heney, well-known for a successful record of convictions of dishonest officials in Oregon, was appointed special prosecutor and Johnson as his assistant.(18)

By 1907 Burns collected enough evidence to take several

of the city officials to trial.   The cases took up most of Johnson's time for the next two years.   As it turned out, the prosecution played an important role in launching his political career.   The trial of Mayor Eugene E. Schmitz was Johnson's first major case in the graft prosecutions.   He presented the opening and closing arguments, both of which were praised by the press for their brilliance and denunciation of the culprits.(18)   A few months later Johnson was dropped from the prosecution team when Heney claimed that high expenditures forced the termination of additional lawyers.   Johnson's son believed that the real reason was Heney's jealousy over the attention the press had given his father.(1)

Johnson returned to private practice and participated briefly in a local election giving a few minor speeches in support of Langdon's reelection for district attorney.   He was not in private practice long, however, before fate offered Johnson his chance.   In November, 1908, during the trial of Abraham Ruef, the most powerful political boss in the city, Heney was shot by an assassin.   Even though Heney survived the incident, he was unable to continue the prosecution, and Johnson was asked to take his place.(19)

Once more Johnson was in the limelight.   He offered his final summation December 9, 1908, painting a grim description of Ruef after the earthquake "bartering away the rights of the city and selling them out, and taking the little messages of love and cheer and help and aid and using them for his bane purposes."(1)   After listening to his speech a reporter from the San Francisco Call wrote that there had never been such a "bitter characterization of the arch criminal as that which furnished the theme for Johnson's closing argument for the state."

Stimulated by their success locally, Johnson and others strove to establish a successful statewide reform organization.   Called the Lincoln-Roosevelt League, it was originally organized in 1907 by two newspaper editors, Edward Dickson of the Los Angeles Express and Chester Rowell of the Fresno Republican.   Johnson often spoke at rallies to gain support.   According to his contemporaries, Johnson was particularly good at attracting attention and generating public interest.   Described as a sort of "western Theodore Roosevelt" Johnson proved to be a dynamic advocate, just the type, according to Chester Rowell, needed for the "first fight."(42)   With his help the group grew to considerable size by 1909.   Rowell was elected president of the league and Johnson elected vice president.   Their primary goal was to end the domination of the Southern Pacific political machine and to initiate progressive reform.(21)

Johnson also represented the Direct Primary League before the State Senate Committee on Election Laws in 1909. Even though his father, who opposed the legislation, controlled the committee, Johnson prevailed; two months later California adopted a direct primary law for the first time in its history.( 18)

## "Kick the Southern Pacific out of Politics:" Johnson for Governor

From 1880 to 1910 the Southern Pacific Railroad Company was unchallenged as the single largest influence in California politics. Its power was so pervasive that the company could almost name and control every candidate for political office from the governor down to local positions. Control was maintained through the use of partisan election laws requiring that every candidate's party be stated and that all candidates be nominated by partisan conventions.

Until 1909 reform elements had been unsuccessful in challenging the Southern Pacific's Political Bureau, the instrument through which it controlled the state's political parties.(43)  With the new Primary Law of 1909, however, the chances for success against the railroad increased considerably.  The new law virtually eliminated nominating conventions and allowed any candidate to run for office, providing he could get enough signatures to be listed on the ballot.  Taking advantage of the new law, the Lincoln-Roosevelt League supported Hiram Johnson for governor, Albert Wallace for lieutenant governor, and forty-nine other candidates for various offices.(15)

Nothing better epitomized the campaign than Johnson's acceptance speech which set the theme of the campaign: "I am going ahead making the fight as a progressive Republican on the Roosevelt lines.  I am going to make this fight in an endeavor to return the government of California to the people and take it away from the political bureau of the Southern Pacific Company."(41)

For several months Johnson hammered away at the Southern Pacific Railroad Company, claiming that anyone who opposed him was aligned with the railroad.  Since the Lincoln-Roosevelt League was in reality a reform movement within the Republican party, the real fight came during the primary election.  Although the conservative newspapers of the state could not agree on which of the four other candidates they supported, they were united against Johnson.  For example, the Los Angeles Times and the San Francisco Chronicle, waged a bitter battle against Johnson.  The Times accused Johnson of being pro-railroad, referring to him as "that son-of-a-grove-johnson [sic]," and charged that if he was elected the Southern Pacific Railroad would "have a friend at court in Old Grove Johnson, whom Hiram will obey as meekly today as he did in his teens."

Angered by the opposition's tactics, Johnson lashed out

against his accusers, bitterly denouncing them. He called Harrison Gray Otis, owner and editor of the Times, "depraved, corrupt, crooked, and putrescent."(18) Using a much more satirical approach against the Chronicle, he opened a speech before an audience of over one thousand by commenting that "tomorrow morning you will read in the San Francisco Chronicle that Hiram Johnson was greeted at Chico with a disappointing audience composed of twenty-six men and three women."(18)

Not all of the newspapers in the state opposed Johnson. He was supported by several major newspapers such as the Los Angeles Express, San Francisco Bulletin, Sacramento Bee, Stockton Record, and Fresno Republican. In an attempt to disassociate him from Grove, these papers published several biographical articles which described his campaign for Clark in Sacramento and how he and his brother had opposed their father.(18)

The early part of the campaign proved to be disastrous. Everyone running on the Lincoln-Roosevelt League ticket wished to travel with Johnson and to speak on the same platform. A lack of organization and leadership caused blunders such as premature or mishandled newspaper stories. The campaign was also plagued by a lack of advance publicity and by a shortage of funds. After a few mistakes and setbacks, Johnson declared that the "Lincoln-Roosevelt League was simply not prepared to wage a statewide campaign supporting a ticket of nearly fifty candidates."(42) With his usual finesse Johnson put the problem in clear perspective: "Of all the Damn Fool Leagues that ever existed, the Lincoln-Roosevelt Republican League not only is the worst, but the worst that could ever be conceived."(42)

Johnson decided that the only sensible alternative was for him personally to take over the management of his campaign. With the help of Al McCabe, his law partner and personal friend, and his loyal secretary, Harriet Odgers, Johnson took control and established his own strategy. To begin with, he refused to allow any other candidates to travel with him. As he wrote in a letter to Rowell: "I do not care to have Mr. Wallace, [his running-mate], and forty-eight other candidates merely seeking office with me on the road."(1) Realizing the importance of the campaign Johnson did not want it "cheapened by a mere scramble for office. . . ."(42)

Johnson's itinerary was determined with the help of a road map, and his son and any reporters who volunteered went ahead to post notices of the time and location of the rally. Upon his arrival his son rang a cowbell attached to the red locomobile. Speaking on small street corners, sometimes to only fifteen or twenty people, he promised to rid politics of the Southern Pacific and its followers.(1)

In focusing on the small rural areas rather than the large population centers, Johnson demonstrated that he had a "shrewd insight into the farm economy and understanding of an important power structure, the rural population."(42)  Most of the ranchers and farmers relied on the railroad to transport their products to market and, at one time or another, had experienced high and discriminatory rates. Thus, Johnson's attack was popular among members of this group who had an economic reason for disliking the railroad.

Like most Progressives Johnson viewed big business as the prime cause of corruption in government.  His denunciations of the large corporations proved popular with the poor and working-class.  As Robert Cleland noted:  "The people saw in him only the fearless nominee of the Lincoln-Roosevelt League, the two-fisted champion of the common man, the California Roosevelt, the nemesis of the political machine."(66)

Johnson's speaking style changed very little during the campaign.  Most of his speeches were repetitious as he hammered away at the railroad and special interests. According to one of his contemporaries his voice had trajectory power, an important characteristic since no public address systems were available in 1910.  While not musical, his voice was deep and had an appealing cadence that seemed to grip and hold attention.  His delivery was rapid, as were his gestures, although they were few in number.  His most common gesture was a downward drive with his right fist into the palm of his other hand, and occasionally he extended both arms toward his audience with open palms.  At other times, he raised his right arm with his index finger upright as if lecturing when making a striking point.(51)

He rarely moved the rest of his body while speaking. Edgar Williams noted that he had seen him speak "for an hour and over without moving from the position first taken, unless it was to take a drink of water."(51)  As for personal appearance, he was described as rather short and stocky with a round florid face which portrayed his "pugnacious character."(41)  These characteristics combined to give his audiences an impression of intensity, and according to one reporter, "a ring of sincerity."(18)

The overall campaign might be properly described as sort of a religious crusade rather than a political campaign.  The Riverside Press reported that his speeches sounded more "like the inspiring appeals of some prophet or crusader of the delivered truth" than a politician seeking office.  Edmund Norton, a writer for La Follette's Magazine, noted that he saw in some of Johnson's audiences a "moral fervor fusing the assemblies into almost a spiritual frenzy for a few seconds; a mass phenomenon . . . rarely or never witnessed outside of religious meetings."(53)  He was characterized as a "political revivalist" by a writer for McClure's.(53)

Interestingly, Johnson, fearing failure, was always nervous and unable to sleep before a major speech, fearing failure. Yet his fears were not well founded. He easily won the primary election. Charles Curry carried San Francisco and Sacramento counties, but Johnson won a total of 101,666 votes, only 12,273 less than the combined total of his four Republican opponents. He did well in the rural areas and in the populated areas of southern California, which gave him one-fifth of his entire statewide vote.(42)

After the primary his strategy remained basically the same, attacking the Southern Pacific and accusing his opponent of conspiring with the railroad. In the final count Johnson defeated his Democratic opponent, Theodore Bell, by a narrow margin of about 22,000 votes. In fact, most of the Lincoln-Roosevelt League candidates won, giving them a clear majority in the legislature. Surprisingly, the total cost of the campaign for the league was only $27,929.79, which included the costs of meetings, publicity, headquarters, election day expenses, and petitions.(18) Johnson must be given a significant degree of the credit. By the end of the campaign he had given a minimum of six hundred speeches and traveled over eight thousand miles, quite a feat when one considers the fact that most of the roads were still unpaved in 1910.(1)

Johnson's first administrative action was to cancel the traditional and elaborate inaugural ball, thus signalling the transfer of the government from the wealthy and privileged class, accustomed to extravagance, back to the common people. Franklin Hichborn recalled that Johnson, like Jefferson, refused the usual inaugural parade and "as a plain American gentleman walked to the Capitol unattended by military escort."(33) Johnson's address, similar to Jefferson's first inaugural, asked that partisanship be forgotten and pleaded for cooperation among the legislators, "not as Republicans or Democrats, but as representatives of all the people of all classes and political affiliations. . . ." In reaffirming his campaign promises, he outlined a reform program and proclaimed that his first duty was "to eliminate every private interest from the government, and to make the public service of the state responsible solely to the people."(37)

In the months that followed, the reforms that Johnson requested were passed by the legislature, and in November, 1911, the initiative, referendum, and recall amendments to the state constitution were submitted to the electorate for approval. By the end of the first year of his administration no less than twenty-three amendments to the state constitution were passed.(53) So effective were his reforms that the state experienced a statewide reduction in railroad rates which was estimated by June, 1912, to have saved shippers, consumers, and the traveling public more than $2,000,000.

Labor benefited most from the Johnson years.  During the
1913 session the Workman's Compensation Insurance and Safety
Act was adopted and three new agencies were created:  the
Industrial Welfare Commission,  Industrial Accident
Commission, and Commission of Immigration and Housing.  Paul
Scharrenberg, secretary of the California State Federation of
Labor,  praised Governor Johnson and declared that his
"uncompromising attitude for an effective Workman's
Compensation Act . . . should ever endear him to the men and
women of labor."(42)  The legislature also passed higher
corporate taxes and created an administrative board to manage
all state institutions.(1)

None of these issues were as pressing as the anti-alien
legislation prohibiting aliens and alien corporations from
owning land in California unless eligible for citizenship.
Farmers were its greatest proponents.  In fact public
sentiment was so widespread that both parties supported anti-
alien legislation;  and even President Wilson declared
approval for a national policy of exclusion during the
campaign.  Similar plans had been considered in previous
sessions, but action had been delayed for various reasons.
Public pressure became so great by 1913, however, that
legislators felt compelled to do something or to face defeat
in the 1914 election.(34)

Following the passing of the anti-alien measure in both
the California House and Senate, President Wilson received a
letter of protest from the Japanese government and learned of
a mass protest in Tokyo.  In a conciliatory effort, Wilson
asked Johnson and the legislature to reconsider the issue.
Johnson replied that the law was in no way discriminatory and
should not antagonize a foreign government.  Wilson then sent
Secretary of State William Jennings Bryan to California to
block the passage of the law, but he offered nothing new and
only managed to irritate Johnson and the legislature by the
delay.  As Johnson said:  "Mr. Bryan presented nothing that
could not have been transmitted within the limits of a night
letter without using all of the allotted words."(34)
Ignoring Bryan's request that nothing be done until he had
had a chance to confer with the president, Johnson signed the
bill into law on May 19, 1913.

Johnson justified his action arguing that the federal
government already had three laws forbidding alien ownership
of land, one applying to the District of Columbia, one to the
territories, and one to the public lands.  Secondly, eight
states (Illinois, Ohio, Kentucky, Oklahoma, Missouri, Texas,
Arizona, and Washington) also had laws prohibiting ownership.
Even Japan had a law prohibiting aliens from owning land.  As
Johnson stated, if the law was discriminatory, it was because
federal law, not state law, prevented certain nationalities
from becoming citizens.  Finally, Johnson pointed out that,
since the Supreme Court had not ruled any of these laws

unconstitutional, California was right to pass such a measure.(34)

In the final analysis, Johnson does not deserve sole blame for the measure. He was only responding to public pressure. The bill had passed both houses almost unanimously, 35 to 2 in the Senate and 72 to 3 in the House. As Johnson said in a statement to Bryan: "With such unanimity of opinion, even did I hold other views, I would feel it my plain duty to sign the bill, unless some absolutely controlling necessity demanded contrary action. Apparently no such controlling necessity exists."(34)

By the end of 1913 Johnson had grown tired of state politics, preferring to run for a national office. Privately, in letters to friends and followers he confided that he did "not care to be governor again." But his close associates, Meyer Lissner and Chester Rowell, convinced him that his resignation as governor would only cause confusion within the movement.(1) So Johnson eventually acquiesced and agreed to run for reelection in 1914.

Repeating his 1910 stump campaign, Johnson easily defeated his Democratic opponent by a good margin, receiving much more of the labor vote. In his inaugural address Johnson praised the legislators for their past performance, summarizing the most notable reforms:

> Boss rule has been made permanently impossible by direct nomination, direct legislation, and the recall.
> Suffrage has been extended to women.
> The elections of judges, school officials and county officers have been made non-partisan.
> The public utilities are controlled and regulated by the State.
> The public business of the State has been centralized and systematized under a Board of Control. School textbooks have been made free of cost to the pupils. A civil service law has destroyed political patronage.
> Prisons and reform schools reflect a humaner [sic] policy. The underlying principle is that the State, while conserving all material interests, first concerns itself with conservation of its humanity. . . .(18)

The 1915 legislature improved the Workman's Compensation Law, removed property qualifications for jury service, established free employment bureaus, and improved child-labor laws.(42) The legislative accomplishments during Johnson's terms as governor must be applauded. He and his supporters directly confronted the problems of corruption in government, railroad domination, labor conditions, education, and other critical issues of their time.

## "A Crusader for a New Cause:"  Johnson for Vice President

Hiram Johnson's overwhelming victory in 1910 and the spectacular reforms by the California legislature during the 1911 session won widespread approval and admiration.  The resulting publicity and the unquestioned control of the state's Republican political organization propelled Johnson and his followers into the national arena of politics, an ambition that they had held since their growing disenchantment with President William Howard Taft.

Taft's failure to pursue progressive reform, evidenced by his support of the Payne-Aldrich Tariff Bill in 1909 and his support during the Alaskan land controversy of Richard Ballenger, secretary of the interior, instead of Gifford Pinchot, chief forester under TR's administration kindled malcontent among the insurgents.(42)  Hoping to purge Taft from the party, they formed the National Progressive Republican League.  It was founded in the home of Senator Robert La Follette from Wisconsin and announced by the nation's press on January 23, 1911.  Hiram Johnson, Edward Dickson, and Chester Rowell, as well as other Progressives from the West Coast were among its charter members.(63)  They pledged themselves to promote progressive ideals in a nationwide campaign and to nominate a progressive candidate in the 1912 presidential election.  Quite naturally, Roosevelt was their favorite, but he refused to be considered.  Senator Albert Cummins from Iowa, Gifford Pinchot, and others were mentioned as potential candidates, but they lacked sufficient support to win the nomination.(15)

With the exception of Roosevelt, only Robert La Follette enjoyed enough popularity to be considered a serious contender.  As one of the founders of the National Progressive Republican League, its leading spokesman and a successful politician, he was a reasonable alternative.  Governor Johnson admired La Follette's successful record, but was not at all convinced that he could defeat Taft.  In one of his many letters to Roosevelt, Johnson pleaded with him to enter the race, arguing that Taft's nomination was almost guaranteed if he ran against La Follette.(1)  Nonetheless, a meeting of California Progressives was called on November 25, 1911.  Still disappointed by Roosevelt's refusal to run, Governor Johnson pledged his support of the newly named "California La Follette League."  The meeting ended with a unanimous call for immediate action.  Enthusiasm must have been half-hearted, however, because there was little evidence of a campaign during the next few weeks.(15)

Two significant factors contributed to the failure of La Follette's campaign in California.  The first was the senator's own doing.  Rather than embarking on a vigorous speaking campaign, La Follette chose to remain in seclusion, writing his autobiography.(63)  Without the senator's active participation the movement did not have enough buoyancy to sustain itself.    A second and more important factor was the changing mood of Theodore Roosevelt.    Within days following the establishment of the La Follette League in California, Roosevelt was writing his closest friends and associates asking them to "sound out the country."    No one could interpret this as anything other than a sign that he was reconsidering running in 1912.    TR added to the suspense by refusing to assure representatives from both Taft and La Follette that he was not a candidate.    His motive finally became transparent in January when he confessed to Johnson that if the nomination was forced on him as "a genuine expression of the popular will, [he] would feel obligated to accept without regard to what the outcome might be."(86)

Roosevelt did not wait long for a "sign" from the people.    A few days following his letter to Johnson, he sent another message requesting the governor to visit him in the East for a discussion on the political situation.(86)    In preparation for the meeting, Johnson met with both Chester Rowell and Meyer Lissner to consider strategies for convincing Roosevelt to enter the race.    This was probably not the only topic they discussed, for they had already pledged their support to La Follette and withdrawing it would be rather embarrassing.    They agreed that Johnson would act on their behalf in pledging support to Roosevelt.    Meanwhile, they would continue to appear to support La Follette until the Colonel's candidacy was announced publicly.(42)

Johnson met with Roosevelt on February 2, 1912.(3e) Soon thereafter Johnson sent a telegram to his friends in California enthusiastically reporting that TR was definitely in the race.(1)    At the same time La Follette seemed to suffer a physical and mental collapse when delivering an address in Philadelphia to the Periodical Publishers Association.    David Thelen suggests in his biography of the senator that a combination of factors was responsible for the collapse: exhaustion from months of campaigning, rumors that Roosevelt would soon announce his own candidacy, and news that his daughter would need a dangerous operation.(63) Nevertheless, the next day the nation's press reported that La Follette had suffered a nervous breakdown.    The New York Times quoted his campaign managers as saying that the senator was withdrawing from the contest.    Even though La Follette later denied this report, the Philadelphia debacle could not have come at a more opportune time for the California Progressives.    On the nineteenth of February, while visiting his son, Archie, in New York, Johnson formally announced to the press that he was switching his support from Senator La Follette to Theodore Roosevelt.(3e)    By this time Roosevelt had issued his "Charter of Democracy" address, prepared with the help of Johnson, before the Ohio constitutional convention.(59)    The speech was a formal announcement of his candidacy and an outline of his political program.

Another movement was initiated while Johnson was in the East. Edwin Earl, owner of the Los Angeles Express and the Morning Tribune, began a campaign in support of Johnson for vice president. Campaigning for the vice presidential nomination was unprecedented in American politics. The Johnson movement was an exception to this tradition. As many editorials pointed out, the proponents hoped that careful selection of a vice president might transform the office into a useful and significant position, one which might influence national policies.(59)

Although Johnson did not campaign on his own behalf, he was aware of the movement and, in fact, encouraged the enterprise. When he heard about the progress of the campaign from Edward Dickson, Washington correspondent for the Express and Tribune, Johnson wrote back that "you have been mighty good and I appreciate it thoroughly." To questions as to whether he would accept the nomination, Johnson replied: "I would be hypocritical if I pretended I would not like the second highest office in this country, and I should be very glad indeed, if the result would be that the nomination would come to me."(1)

Dickson was already attempting to gain support for the governor from other newspapers in the nation and endorsements from such well-known Progressives as Gifford Pinchot, Mark Sullivan and Medill McCormick. Earl wrote to Roosevelt that with Johnson as a running-mate, the campaign slogan "Hands across the Continent" would carry them to victory.(59) A day after his letter to the Colonel, Earl devoted half the front page of the Express to the campaign. It was filled with pictures of Roosevelt and Johnson along with an editorial declaring:

> As Roosevelt has battled against special privilege and privilege interest in government of the republic, so has Johnson fought it, with splendor of courage and unparalleled success in the State. As Johnson kicked the Southern Pacific out of the Republican party and out of the government of the State, so will Roosevelt and Johnson kick plutocracy out of the Republican party and out of the government of the nation.(59)

Other progressive Republican newspapers and periodicals joined the crusade. The California Outlook placed pictures of the two candidates on the covers of the February 24 and March 2 issues. The Venice Daily Vanguard referred to the possible union as a "mighty strong team" which would lead to a victory for the common people. Outside the state, several newspapers such as the Washington Times and the Chicago Evening Post supported Johnson's candidacy.

Such support was not unanimous, however. Conservative papers ridiculed the Johnson movement. The San Bernardino Sun, for example, claimed that there was no more "possibility of Governor Johnson being the Republican nominee for vice president than there was in his being made minister to Mars." Other papers believed the campaign to be a "shallow and transparent trick" to gain support for Roosevelt. The San Francisco Evening Post accused Johnson and his associates of bartering votes in California in exchange for the vice presidential nomination.

On March 11, 1912, in Los Angeles, Governor Johnson officially began the presidential campaign for Roosevelt in California. Local newspapers reported that, despite a heavy rain, Johnson attracted a capacity crowd to hear him proclaim that "this battle is the age-long battle of privilege against common welfare" and that "a great movement . . . is in the balance."(3i)

The California presidential preference primary was held May 14, 1912. Two weeks earlier, in a final effort to guarantee victory, Johnson was joined by Gifford Pinchot and Senator Albert Beveridge of Indiana for a statewide speaking tour. The campaign resulted in a decisive victory for Roosevelt. The ex-president received more than double the votes collected by Taft and more votes than the president and La Follette combined.(42)

Of the twelve northern and western states with direct primaries, Roosevelt won nine, carrying California, Illinois, Maryland, Nebraska, Oregon, South Dakota, Pennsylvania, New Jersey, and Taft's home state of Ohio. Taft won only Massachusetts by a very small margin. La Follette carried North Dakota and his home state, Wisconsin, where he faced no opposition. In terms of popular votes, TR was easily the favorite. In fact, the total vote cast in the primaries gave La Follette 351,043, Taft 761,716, and Roosevelt an impressive 1,157,397.(56)

From these states, Roosevelt won 278 delegates compared to 36 for La Follette and 48 for Taft. Of the 1,078 delegates attending the Republican convention, the remaining 716 were chosen by a variety of means, including caucuses, state conventions, and conferences, none of which allowed voters a direct means of expressing their preferences. Through a series of controversial and questionable practices, Taft claimed a majority of the nonprimary delegates.(56) The Roosevelt forces, however, refused to acknowledge the validity of the results.

By the time the Republican National Committee convened on June 7, 1912, over 254 delegates seats were being contested by opposing factions. Of those challenged, two were from California. State law provided for the election of delegates by the state at large while party rules dictated that they be determined by individual congressional districts. The controversy concerned the San Francisco district where Taft forces claimed a majority. Recent changes in the boundary lines, however, confused the issue. Even the city registrar of voters was unable to testify with any confidence as to who had received the majorities in the disputed district.(15)

Francis Heney unsuccessfully represented the California Progressives before the National Committee. With the Taft forces solidly in control of the committee the outcome was foreordained. Of the 254 contested seats Taft was awarded 235, including the two California seats, while Roosevelt received only 19.(56) Johnson was invited by the committee to attend the proceedings during the discussion of the California question, but refused on the grounds that he would "not submit to a trial to the title of property by the thief who steals it."(3d) His accusation was not necessarily unwarranted. Observers of the proceedings generally agreed that according to party rules and accepted standards of adjudication Roosevelt should have received more delegates than he was awarded. Governor Herbert Hadley of Missouri and Senator William E. Borah of Idaho, TR supporters, estimated that he should have won approximately fifty of the challenged seats.(56) Others have concurred with these estimates, among them, Gilbert E. Roe, a writer for La Follette's Weekly (a publication clearly hostile to the Colonel) and George Mowry, the respected historian of the period.(15)

When the final tally was completed, it was clear that the Taft forces would enjoy a majority at the convention, more than enough to guarantee his nomination. As Johnson was preparing to depart for Chicago, he sent telegrams to both his son, Hiram, Jr., and Meyer Lissner predicting that "I think we may preside at the historic birth of the Progressive Party."(1)

The evening prior to the opening of the convention, Roosevelt inspired a large and already enthusiastic crowd with words of encouragement and an outline of the ideals for which they labored. The address was given in the Chicago Auditorium. He concluded:

Here in Chicago, at this time, you have a great task before you. I wish you to realize deep in your hearts that you are not merely facing a crisis in the history of a party. You are facing a crisis in the nation. . . . We fight in an honorable fashion for the good of mankind; fearless of the future; unheeding of our individual fates; with unflinching hearts and undimmed eyes; we stand at Armageddon, and we battle for the Lord.(56)

The stage was set. The scene was the Republican convention with the scenario following the pattern of a classic tale of good battling against the evil forces of greed and corruption. The villains were played by the Taft delegates, led by Boies Penrose of Pennsylvania and William Barnes of New York. Through treachery and dirty tricks, they intended to rob Roosevelt, depicted as the champion of the people, of his rightful nomination. The good guys were played by the Progressives led by Governor Johnson of California, Albert Beveridge of Indiana, and William E. Borah of Idaho. Awarded the honor of presenting Roosevelt's seconding speech, Johnson would be at center stage to point an accusing finger at the villains as they committed their infamous crime. There would be shouts from the galleries and the nation's press, witness to the "theft," would demand justice. And then, as if by divine right, Roosevelt would enter with a new script outlining the formation of a new party with the primary goal of returning the government back to the people. The country would thus be saved from the evil forces of big business.

The curtain rose on June 18, 1912, as the convention was called to order. The proceedings were anything but orderly. Tempers flared, insults were shouted, and demonstrations occurred both on the floor and in the galleries. There were also reports of fist fights between delegates. Meanwhile, the streets were filled with crowds cheering and waving banners. The first order of business was the selection of chairman. Elihu Root of New York, a Taft supporter, was selected by a margin of twenty-nine votes.( 3e) It was a major blow to the Progressives.

In order to prevent the Taft forces from completely dominating the convention, the Progressives turned to the credentials committee as a court of last appeal. Governor Johnson led the fight. Protesting the selection of the convention chairman, he declared: "We deny the right of any moribund National Committee to choose our Chairman for us . . . and we deny the right of any set of men to Mexicanize the Republican Party. . . ." As Johnson spoke he was hissed by the Taft supporters and according to the New York Times, as a result, "the more defiant his utterances became." Twice during the next twenty-four hours Johnson led his troops out of the hall in protest against an unfavorable decision.

By the afternoon of June 20 it was obvious that the Taft forces had won. Root was installed as chairman and the Progressives were defeated on every important issue, including a motion to bar the contested delegates from voting. That evening a conference was held at the Roosevelt headquarters to discuss bolting the convention. Governors Stubbs, Aldrich, Hadley, and Glasscock opposed bolting on the grounds that there was too much to lose and that there were too many difficulties in organizing a new party. Irritated by their reluctance, Johnson complained: "We are frittering away our time. We are frittering away our opportunity. And what is worse, we are frittering away Theodore Roosevelt." The deadlock was finally broken toward morning by the pledges of publisher Frank Munsey and financier George Perkins to guarantee substantial financial support.( 56) Before a group of supporters in the hotel Johnson declared:

> We are going to stop dilly-dallying with this robbing
> convention.  We are going in there to fight, and we are
> prepared for the birth of a new Republican party.  This
> new party, which is inevitable, will not countenance
> robbery,  thievery  and  dishonesty  such  as  we  have
> experienced here.(18)

With  secession  imminent  Johnson  arrived  at  the
convention to present his final denunciation of the Taft
forces.  Aiming  his  rhetoric  at  the  opposition,  Johnson  spoke
with vehemence and confidence:

> Not only was a fraudulent roll call foisted on us to
> defeat the people's will, but the law of the State of
> California. . . . As California Governor, I feel my duty
> plain--to remain no longer in the convention. . . . The
> struggle is on, North, East, South, and West, for direct
> primaries, and the people all over the country will soon
> be given the right to choose their own representatives
> rather than let the bosses choose them. . . .(3e)

The New York Times reported that when Johnson's twenty
minutes were up, he "stepped back while the crowd, . . . on
its feet, yelled for him to continue.  William Jennings Bryan
led  the  applause,  which  kept  up  for  several  minutes."
Describing the impact of Johnson's speech, Bryan, attending
the convention as a reporter, wrote that the governor "was
the  hero  of  the  day."   What impressed him the most about
Johnson's speech was that it had "the ring of sincerity" and
"convinced the audience that he had justice on his side, but
the  audience  was  not  in  a  position  to  follow  its
convictions."(54)   A  writer  for  Current  Literature  provided
the most memorable description of Johnson's style:

> No one who attended the Chicago convention this year can
> ever forget that voice.  It has no honey in it.  It is a
> fighting voice, and when Johnson is mad--as he was all
> the time at Chicago--it sounds like a ripsaw going
> through a hard knot.  Terse is the word for it.  There is
> no ease in his platform manner, no attempt to ingratiate
> himself,   no   pleasant   smile   or   suggestion   of
> jocularity. . . . Johnson never smiled.  The first notes
> of his voice keyed up your nerves to a fighting pitch.
> We can't imagine anyone's listening to Johnson for five
> minutes without wanting to fight--either to fight with or
> to fight against him.  His voice sounds just as an east
> wind feels.  It grates and snarls and pierces, and puts
> you all on edge.  The whole man goes with the voice.
> Every posture and gesture is one of intensity.  His hands
> are nearly always clenched.  His jaw, a good strong
> fighting jaw, is set.  His muscles are tense.  He talks
> rapidly and with no gradation of volume or tone, without
> any embellishments of rhetoric, without any appearance of

self-consciousness.  He gives you the impression of a man
carried away entirely on the flood of his own
feelings.(53)

The San Francisco Argonaut described Johnson's behavior
from the opposition's point of view:

How pitifully small appears this little coxcomb in his
efforts to strut and pose in the turmoil of large
affairs!
    From start to finish he played the part of a mean-
spirited, bad tempered, spoiled boy, minus manner, minus
fairness, minus poise, minus any trace of manly dignity
or grace.(18)

Johnson's address was a formal vindication of the
Progressives' secession from the Republican party.  Shortly
thereafter, Johnson led his followers out of the convention
for the final time.  William Howard Taft was renominated by a
vote of 561 to 107 for Roosevelt, 41 for La Follette, 17 for
Cummins, and 2 for Hughes.  Of the remaining delegates, 344
refused to vote.(3e)  That evening most of them were at
Orchestra Hall listening to Johnson present the opening
address at the rump convention instead of the seconding
speech he never made at the Republican convention.

In a more sober tone than in his previous speech Johnson
warned his audience of the difficulties they faced.  He said:
"Everyone who embarks in this course understands full well
the responsibility which is his and recognizes the obstacles
to overcome."  Their future, Johnson explained, rested with
the hope that, "whenever there is a great wrong to be
righted, the people will take up the fight and win."(3e)

The Colonel followed Johnson to the podium, declaring
that he would only accept the nomination from the group if it
was the result of an official convention, properly called and
held in the traditional manner.  He asked them to return to
their respective states, "to sound out the country," and then
to return in a few weeks to make their nominations.  The
convention was scheduled for early August.(3e)

Meanwhile Johnson was made temporary chairman in charge
of organizing the new convention.  Honored by his new role
and enthusiastic about the new movement, Johnson boarded the
train for California.  However, his optimism was somewhat
premature because the initial reaction was not encouraging.
Many leading Republican politicians listed as prominent
Progressives refused to join the new party.  The press
reported, for example, that Governor Hadley of Missouri and
Governor Osborn of Michigan, both original Roosevelt
supporters, refused to join.  The most significant
Progressive missing was none other than Senator
Robert La Follette, and without his endorsement the new party
failed to attract other prominent liberals such as Rudolph

Spreckels and Charles Crane, important financial backers.(56)

The coup de grace came on July 2 during the Democratic National Convention.  The Progressives had hoped that the Democrats would nominate a conservative, forcing the liberal faction into the Progressive camp.  Instead, on the forty-sixth ballot, fearing that the progressive faction might bolt, enough conservatives switched to Governor Woodrow Wilson of New Jersey, a well-known liberal, giving him the nomination.  Governor Thomas R. Marshall of Indiana, describing himself as "a progressive with the brakes on" was chosen for vice president.(3e)  With Wilson as the Democratic nominee, the Progressives could expect little support from liberal Democrats.

The first Progressive National Convention opened August 5, 1912, in Chicago.  Senator Albert Beveridge of Indiana opened the proceedings with a stirring address before a cheering audience.  Roosevelt then issued his "Confession of Faith" which amounted to a denunciation of the Republican party and an outline of radical reform.  He called for a national preferential primary, direct election of senators, prohibition of child labor, women's suffrage, a minimum wage, eight-hour work days, regulation of monopolies and trusts, conservation of natural resources, protective tariffs, and a graduated inheritance tax.(1)

The next order of business was the selection of candidates.  Roosevelt was already considered the presidential nominee, of course, but the vice presidential candidate had not been determined.  Believing the campaign hopeless, most declined.  Even Johnson, one of the founders of the party, was reluctant to accept the position.  He eventually acquiesced, but not until he was assured that all other candidates had withdrawn.(15)  In a letter to W. F. Chandler he explained:

> I . . . declined until the night before the nomination. When they put it up to me that one man was giving his all to that fight; that with his glorious past he did not shrink from a humiliating defeat, and that where others were demanded they should yield, I felt I should do my part.(1)

On August 7, 1912, Senator Albert Beveridge announced to an enthusiastic crowd the nominations of Theodore Roosevelt and Hiram Johnson as the first candidates of the National Progressive Party.  With so much excitement and enthusiasm present, there was little evidence of the imminent defeat that experts were predicting.  Johnson declared realistically as he accepted the nomination:  "I would rather go down to defeat with that man, [pointing at Roosevelt] than to go to victory with any other Presidential candidate."(3e)  The declaration, while prophetic, still brought audience members to their feet cheering for their nominees.  Perhaps the best description of the convention was given by William Henry Harbaugh who predicted prior to its meeting that it was destined to be "a failure of politics and a triumph of ideals."( 18)

The next day Johnson returned to California to begin his campaign at Dreamland Rink in San Francisco.  To the 12,000 cheering supporters welcoming him home, Johnson described the delegates to the National Progressive Convention as "carrying a Bible in one hand and a claymore in the other."  In describing himself, he said: "To you I appear just as I hope in the next sixty days in this nation to be, a crusader for a new cause."  Furthermore, Johnson declared, "we are going to forget in a national contest how to make men richer, and we are going to try to make men better."(1)

Despite the optimism of his rhetoric, Johnson was under no illusions as to what the final outcome of the 1912 campaign would be.  To W. F. Chandler he wrote:

> Somebody, in a movement of this sort, has to pioneer the way, and if the sacrifices are made with the sort of contest we are about to commence, the harvest will be gathered four years hence.  I have the feeling this year that "The Blood of the Martyr will be the seed of the Church."(1)

During the next few weeks Johnson made a gallant effort. Following the San Francisco address he embarked on a ten-week speaking tour during which he traveled to twenty-two states delivering over 500 speeches.(42)  In Lincoln, Nebraska, he met with William Jennings Bryan, who, while campaigning for Wilson, told an audience of 10,000 that Johnson was "the biggest man in the Progressive movement," a man that he would rather have as president than Roosevelt.  In Illinois, Johnson followed the trail of the historic Lincoln-Douglas debates. Against allegations that the Progressive party would spell the end of free enterprise, he emphasized in Freeport that "we do not mean to destroy business, but we do not wish the government to devote its entire time to swelling fortunes.  A government which devotes all of its time to the development of business is worse than no government."(3g)

The East, especially New York, Johnson found to be the most disappointing part of the campaign.  Following his speaking tour, he complained to E. A. Van Valkenberg, a Progressive from Ohio, that the management of the campaign in New York was intolerable and that "unless a revolution took place, I would not think of returning . . . and I am not sure I could return if one were to occur."(1)  In fact, he was so upset about the way he had been treated by the party leaders in New York that he threatened to quit the campaign.  It was only through the intervention of his friends that Johnson was persuaded to meet the engagements that they scheduled for him.(15)

Johnson found the 1912 campaign to be a disheartening experience. Although the audiences were generally large and enthusiastic, Johnson received little coverage from the press. He discovered, as many vice presidential candidates have, that running-mates seldom make headlines. Perhaps even more disturbing to Johnson was the treatment he received from his own party. While Roosevelt was afforded a private rail car and assigned a whole battery of publicity men, Johnson was forced to travel in a public Pullman without the aid of a single press agent. He complained to the party headquarters that he was often forced to make his own reservations.(15) Johnson concluded that the whole campaign had been mismanaged, which was not surprising when one considers the length of time that the party had existed. John Gable, a scholar of the period, identified a few of the problems they faced which included contacting local leaders, recruiting district and precinct captains, renting office space, arranging publicity, preparing campaign material, recruiting and organizing a whole host of speakers, and financing the campaign.(56)

As experts predicted, Wilson won the election. Roosevelt carried Pennsylvania, Michigan, Minnesota, South Dakota, Washington, and California by a slim margin of 174 votes. Taft won only Utah and Vermont, and Wilson carried the rest of the nation. The Progressives were weakest in the South where they had little organization or support. Neither Johnson nor Roosevelt spent much time campaigning there which may have contributed to their weakness. In terms of popular votes, Wilson received 6,301,254, Roosevelt 4,127,788, and Taft only 3,485,831. In New York, where Johnson had bitterly complained about the campaign, Roosevelt received 382,672, compared to 647,994 for Wilson. Overall, Wilson won 435 electoral votes, Roosevelt 88, and Taft 8.(56)

Johnson's greatest contribution was his rhetorical ability. He proved to be a vigorous campaigner, capable of attracting large audiences which usually came away supportive of the Progressive ticket. It is not surprising that in every national election prior to his death presidential candidates solicited his support and asked him to campaign for them. Johnson's speeches during the campaign symbolized the Progressive philosophy. He argued for a strong federal government geared toward regulating business for the purpose of redistributing the wealth in the nation. Johnson also overcame the barrier of geography. It was the first time that a major candidate came from the West.

The Progressives won a greater percentage of the vote than had any other third party movement. Of the three major parties, the Progressives spent the least, amounting to $676,672.73 compared to $1,159,446.36 for the Democrats and $1,076,391.51 for the Republicans.(131) From a purely financial standpoint, the Progressives got more for their money, having spent less per vote than either of the two major parties.

The future of the Progressive party, despite its strong showing in 1912, was short-lived. Frank Munsey, one of the major financial backers, withdrew his support, and there were reports that many of the rank and file were leaving the party. Nevertheless, Johnson remained hopeful. He wrote to George Perkins that: "We still have many captains and commanders, and if we can hold together these officers, we may forget and make our opponents forget the rank and file."(1) It was too late, however, because by late 1915 it was evident that Roosevelt did not intend to run in 1916 as the Progressive candidate. Some Progressives such as E. M. Lee, chairman of the Progressive Committee in Indiana, wrote Johnson asking him to run, but Johnson declined. As Johnson told C. S. Bird from Massachusetts: "There is just one outstanding American today, just one man who approaches greatness as all of us have dreamed of it; just one who can uphold and express the Americanism that all of us feel, and that is Roosevelt." Johnson only hoped that Roosevelt would delay announcing his decision long enough so that they would "be able to compel a decent nominee in the Republican Party."(1)

In June, 1916, the National Progressive Convention was held in Chicago at the same time as the National Republican Convention. The Progressives were loyally supporting Roosevelt even though he had made it clear that he would not accept the nomination unless it was from the Republican party. Representatives from both parties met to discuss the possibility of reaching some sort of compromise hoping to prevent the disaster that occurred in 1912. Unable to surrender their ideals, the Progressives went ahead and nominated Roosevelt, but on June 10, he formally declined the nomination.(62) The episode was a bitter blow to the Progressives and they disbanded without nominating a presidential candidate.

Meanwhile, in order to placate the returning Progressives, the Republican National Convention nominated Charles Evans Hughes for president. He was from New York where he had compiled an impressive record as governor. As a moderate, he appealed to many of the Progressives. On June 12, 1916, Johnson met with Hughes at the Hotel Astor in Chicago and pledged his support in the coming election.(42) Perhaps Johnson summed up his position best when he told reporters in Chicago that: "We are in a difficult position, but we are used to fighting. We will continue to fight on the West Coast."(18) Johnson returned to California leaving the Progressive party behind him. He advised his followers to register in the major parties but to continue the progressive fight whenever possible. Johnson also decided to resign as governor and to run for the U.S. Senate.

## Back in the Republican Party: Johnson for Senator

Johnson officially opened his campaign for senator at the Trinity Auditorium in Los Angeles, July 22, 1916.(3g)  He then followed a trail similar to his 1910 gubernatorial campaign, speaking in the small towns of the mother lode in Sonoma, Tuolumine, and Jackson counties as well as in the larger cities.  Generally, the newspapers reported warm and enthusiastic audiences.  It was an inexpensive campaign.  In fact, to a supporter offering money, Johnson refused, replying:  "I make probably the most economical campaign.  I go into various communities and talk to as many people as possible."(1)

Johnson's closest election was the Republican primary in which he defeated Willis Booth by only 15,064 votes.  In the general election, however, Johnson won by a margin of nearly 300,000.  Hughes, on the other hand, failed to carry the state by about 4,000 votes.(42)  As a result, conservative Republicans accused Johnson of being responsible for the Republican defeat.  These claims, however, were untrue.

Hughes was primarily responsible for his own defeat. Johnson publicly endorsed Hughes on June 27, 1916, and wrote his supporters that he had been speaking on Hughes's behalf.(1)  Hughes, on the other hand, did not offer a similar endorsement of Johnson as he toured the state during the Republican primary.  Instead, Hughes followed the advice of his managers and ignored Johnson and the California Progressives.  He believed what he had been told by members of the old guard that the power and influence of the Johnson forces was no longer significant and, therefore, that any association with them would only hurt his own chances.  As the results indicate, this was not the case.(42)

Despite Hughes's refusal to endorse Johnson, the Progressives might still have been willing to campaign on his behalf had it not been for two incidents.  The first involved Mrs. Johnson.  To Van Valkenberg, a writer for the Philadelphia North American, Johnson complained:  "I tell you confidentially, they forbade Mrs. Johnson to be permitted upon the platform.  It was publicly stated in the shops at San Francisco that she would not be invited to a luncheon given to Mrs. Hughes."(1)

The second and more publicized incident occurred at the Hotel Virginia in Long Beach.  Allegedly, Hughes refused to acknowledge or to greet Johnson even though they were both visiting the hotel.  Later, after the press reported the "snub," Hughes claimed that he was not aware that Johnson was at the hotel.  Although unlikely, Hughes could have made an effort to correct any misunderstandings by personally inviting Johnson to speak at one of his rallies.  The fact that he did not adds evidence to the allegation that it was

not accidental.   Given these facts, it is not surprising that
many Progressives made little effort on Hughes's behalf.(42)

Johnson's election to the U.S. Senate marked the end of
the progressive movement in California.   Clearly, he was the
key figure in the movement.   Without his oratorical
abilities, the movement in California lost much of its
dynamism.   On March 15, 1917, Johnson presented his farewell
address to the California legislature.   It was one of
Johnson's most eloquent speeches and it summarized his
gubernatorial career.   He praised the legislators for their
accomplishments, entrusting them with the future of the
state.   As Johnson ended, his eyes were filled with tears.
He concluded:

> I am loth to say goodbye!   "The mystic chords of memory"
> swell within me.   Each successive step of our advance
> passes in review as I stand before you, the first feeble
> but determined efforts against an oligarchy that had made
> of our wondrous State a railroad satrapy, the militant,
> aggressive attack, the revolution that made us free, the
> consecration and dedication which set our faces to the
> light dimly seen afar, and finally a great people
> emerging out of political bondage to independence and
> freedom.   We have fought the good fight and we have won.
> The victory and its fruits I leave you.
>      May God give you the vision and the firmness and the
> courage to keep the faith!(1)

## Johnson as an Irreconcilable: Against Wilson and the League

When President Woodrow Wilson called the U.S. Senate
into special session in March, 1917, one of the newly elected
members was Hiram Johnson.   Listening carefully to Wilson's
war message, Johnson noted that toward the end of his speech
the president assured the Congress:

> We are glad . . . to fight . . . for the ultimate peace
> of the world. . . .   Its peace must be planted upon the
> tested foundations of political liberty.   We have no
> selfish ends to serve.   We desire no conquest, no
> dominion.   We seek no indemnities for ourselves, no
> material compensation for the sacrifice we shall freely
> make.   We are but one of the champions of the rights of
> mankind. . . .(91)

Johnson fully accepted these goals with the "highest of
motives" and gave his uncompromising support to the president
for all that he asked from Congress to end the war.(75)   With
the coming of peace, however, Johnson's support quickly
dwindled for two reasons:   First, Johnson grew doubtful of
the true motives for which the war had been fought as he saw
certain businessmen reap tremendous profits from the war
effort.   Second, the president's Fourteen Point Address of

January 8, 1918, convinced him that the war was not being waged for righteous reasons. Following the address, Johnson complained to his eldest son:

> Had I stood in the United States Senate when the war was declared, and said we were sending our young men to Europe to give Trieste and the Trentino to Italy, together with a couple of Grecian Islands; that the best blood of America was to be sent in recovering for France, Alsace and Lorraine, in wresting from Austria a national autonomy for a little group of unpronounceable--and until this war, unheard of--races, I would have been confined in an insane asylum, or lashed with scorn from the Senate. . . . We seem to have forgotten making the world safe for democracy. I am very sorry because I did love the phrase.(1)

In analyzing the president's motives, Johnson wrote that Wilson sees himself "as the savior of mankind, and as a ruler who freed all nations, and established world democracy."(1)

In November, 1918, the Germans signed the Armistice accepting Wilson's Fourteen Points as a basis for peace. Commenting on the Peace Commission appointed by President Wilson, Johnson declared publicly that: "There is no God but God, and Mohammed is his prophet. In selecting himself as the head of the five American [member] delegation to the Peace Conference, President Wilson has named himself five times."(89) Despite his opinion of Wilson and the fact that many senators were publicly attacking the treaty, Johnson remained silent. He felt, as he explained to his sons, restrained "because we are yet wholly in ignorance of Wilson's position, and any utterance upon the subject, of which he is champion now, might be at variance with his subsequent determination.(1)

Although Johnson did not take a position against the treaty, he did denounce Wilson several times between December 1918, and June 1919, for the secrecy of the conference and for U.S. involvement in Russian affairs.(243) According to Johnson, America had no business involving itself in the internal affairs of another country. To C. K. McClatchy, Johnson explained his purpose:

> I was endeavoring to point concretely what the League of Nations really is, because, in the Russian situation, we have exactly the League of Nations. This League decreed the Russian expedition against our vote. Congress never declared war, a war has been carried on by the United States troops under the direction and command of the foreign nations, who constitute the majority of the present allied council. . . . If the people could be made to understand a concrete instance like this, and that it is exactly what will be done under a League of Nations, the most forcible example possible, it seems to

me  is  presented.(1)

By January 1919, Johnson had become totally disillusioned.
The president had not kept the negotiations public, nor was
he living up to the aims established in his war message.
Hints of Johnson's noninterventionist philosophy were evident
in all of his speeches.  Johnson declared that "It is time
for an American policy.  Bring home American soldiers.
Rescue our democracy.  Restore its free expression.  Get
American business into its normal channels.  Let American
life, social and economic, be American again."(246)

    In March Johnson officially confirmed himself as a
member of the opposition when he joined with thirty-seven
Republican senators in a petition declaring that they would
not vote for the treaty in its present form.(89)  On May 7,
1919, a summary of the treaty was finally published.  By this
time Wilson had called the Congress into special session.
Johnson delivered his first speech in opposition to the
League of Nations, June 2, 1919.  The United States, Johnson
argued, would bear the burden of defending the territorial
gains of its allies which he described as "national
bankrupts."  Concluding his remarks Johnson said:

> In a word, Mr. President, this League means that American
> boys shall police the world; that all the tottering
> nations of the earth shall be upheld by our blood and our
> bone; that Europe, Asia, and Africa may draw upon us in
> their every dispute and quarrel; that our Nation will be
> at the mercy of European and Japanese diplomats who never
> had and never will have any sympathy with our aspirations
> or our ideals; that we with our glorious past shall
> guarantee the territorial integrity of every country on
> earth and the bondage of every suffering people in
> anguish begging for freedom; that we destroy our Monroe
> Doctrine and submit controversies on the American
> Hemisphere to determination by foreign powers.  It means
> that I must abandon the lessons of my youth, which until
> this moment have been the creed of my manhood, of
> American ideals, American principles, and American
> patriotism; that I must deny the Americanism I taught my
> children, and that under God's blessing I hope to teach
> my grandchildren.  It means the halting and betrayal of
> New World liberalism, the humiliation and end of American
> idealism. . . .  The issue is America. And I am an
> American.(249)

    Johnson's passionate plea is representative of a
unilateralist philosophy and has an enduring quality that
resembles the rhetoric of the Vietnam War era.  The speech
was met with immediate applause from the floor and the
gallery; and no senator arose in refutation.

    Pleased by the response to his speech, Johnson decided
to go on the stump.  He opened his campaign in Carnegie Hall,

New York City, June 28, 1919. The New York Times reported that Johnson evoked hisses at the mere mentioning of Wilson. In a Fourth of July speech before the members of the 339th Infantry in Detroit, Johnson emphasized Americanism, claiming that "we are standing at the crossroads, and one leads to imperialistic control, and the other is the straight and narrow path of Americanism."(3e)

Two days later Johnson addressed the populace of Providence, Rhode Island. The Providence Daily Journal reported that Johnson "stirred his audience of more than 2,000 persons to a wild pitch of enthusiasm."(18) After speaking in Boston the Boston Herald reported that "Senator Johnson was given a vociferous reception. He was cheered and cheered, and cheers were finally called for the "next President" and given without stint.(91) Overall, Johnson was very happy with his short tour through the New England states and bragged to Alex McCabe that it was the most successful tour of all his associates and that it demonstrated a large anti-League sentiment in the country.(1)

On August 27, 1919, President Wilson announced that he would tour the country in support of the League of Nations. Prompted by the Senate's excessive delay, he hoped that public pressure created by his campaign would force them into action. Instead of increasing support, however, the campaign proved to be a futile and desperate failure. Even before Wilson boarded his luxuriously equipped train at Union Station, September 3, 1919, opposing forces were developing plans to neutralize his crusade for the League.(1)

With the support of Senators McCormick and Borah, Johnson decided on a counter-campaign against the president. Never speaking on the same platform, Johnson trailed the president through nineteen states and spoke to as many as 20,000 people in a single day.(3k) Wilson's arguments reflected an optimism about world cooperation and were moralistic in form, revealing an extreme faith in the higher motives of men. Johnson's arguments, on the other hand, were highly pessimistic, revealing a distrust of European diplomacy and a conviction that wars are the result of man's greed and lust for power.

The campaigns stimulated great interest, so much in fact, that the San Francisco Bulletin asserted that the president's "running debate" with Hiram Johnson "transcends" all great forensic encounters "since the memorable Lincoln-Douglas Battle." President Wilson opened his campaign in Columbus, Ohio, September 4, 1919. Johnson followed a few days later, opening September 10, 1919, in Chicago, Illinois. At the very moment that the president was applauding the end of the war to end all wars, Johnson declared, "American boys were upon the Rhine condemned to remain there for fifteen years by virtue of his action. . . . As he uttered his words, seven thousand American sons were being ordered by the

Paris conference, to patrol the coal mines of Silesia." In addition, American boys were being "slain in Asia, at Vladivostok and in Siberia."(3k)

To accusations by Wilson that the opposition were "contemptible quitters" for "not seeing the game through," Johnson asked: "To what 'game' does Mr. Wilson refer? Is it the game he started to play in Europe and did not finish, or is it the game that was played for him and in which finally he supinely acquiesced?" Answering these claims Johnson proudly proclaimed: "The American people are not quitters. They rose majestically and won a great war." They were ready to stand behind Wilson at Paris, "no matter what it cost."(3i) "Who quit the game," he asked? "Wilson," came the roar from the galleries!

Although Wilson and Johnson never actually faced each other on the same platform, their sequential speeches during the rival campaigns took on many aspects of a real debate. Opposition newspaper accounts described Wilson's speaking tour as a total failure. Newspapers favorable toward the League such as the New York Times, observed that people seemed confused and unsure of what the treaty and the League really obligated the United States to do. On the other hand, Johnson captured the sympathy of his audiences. The Washington Herald observed:

> It was evident tonight at Tomlison Hall that the President did not convert permanently all of the city to his point of view. Senator Johnson of California, delivering his second address on his speaking campaign on behalf of the Senate reservationists, obtained from his audience definitely expressed agreement.

Sam Blair, staff correspondent for Universal Service, interviewed several people following Johnson's speech in St. Louis and reported that those who had agreed with Wilson when he spoke in St. Louis admitted that "they had not realized 'exactly what the League would do to the United States.'"(91) Several newspaper accounts reported that Johnson drew slightly larger audiences than the president and received more enthusiastic responses.(91) Following the League's rejection by the Senate, Albert J. Beveridge, a well-known Progressive from Indiana, concluded that Johnson's effort "throughout the country was the last necessary influence" that guaranteed the eventual defeat of the treaty.(1)

In his perceived role as the "American Conscience," Johnson convinced a willing population that the only sensible alternative was that the United States should not become a party to these agreements and that America's rejection of the treaty symbolized a protest against European duplicity. Nothing more dramatically expressed the difference between the opposing ideologies of internationalism and unilateralism than the debate between Johnson and Wilson. The choice was made, and by the end of the rival campaigns the American public clearly preferred to stay out of European affairs.

## "The Issue is America and I am an American:" Johnson for President

Between 1916 and 1924 Hiram Johnson was considered by many as one of the leading contenders for the presidency. His popularity as a Progressive and his nomination in 1912 as Teddy Roosevelt's running-mate in the Bull Moose party brought him an offer to be the 1916 presidential nominee. Discouraged by his 1912 experience and believing its future doomed, Johnson declined the offer.

Three years later, encouraged by the enthusiastic audiences that he had encountered during his anti-League campaign, Johnson reconsidered his chances for the presidency. Typically, Johnson entered the race reluctantly, believing that a conspiracy of wealthy and powerful men would again rob him of victory. His only hope was in winning enough public support to force the party bosses to award him the nomination. Johnson also believed that the party leaders were encouraging as many candidates as possible to enter the race in an effort to prevent him or any other person from gaining enough delegates to win the nomination. As early as February, Johnson predicted that, if successful, they would nominate "somebody of the character of Harding."(1)

Johnson officially announced his candidacy December 13, 1919. As the campaign unfolded, a clear picture of his presidential image and strategy emerged. One of the first primaries he entered was South Dakota. Governor Frank Lowden from Illinois and General Leonard Wood from Indiana, an old friend of Theodore Roosevelt, relied on well-financed media campaigns rather than on personal appearances. Lacking campaign funds, Johnson used information on the amount of money his opponents were spending as one of his campaign issues and continually reminded his audiences of his own poverty. He was backed by "no great corporation, no trust, no powerful financial interests" and God had given only him "against the wealth, the influence and the power of organized politics and organized big business in politics. . . ."(18)

During the campaign Johnson renewed his belief in a conspiracy of special interests against the common man, a common theme he used in 1910 and 1912. As he repeatedly reminded his audiences, "My own poverty-stricken campaign makes an appeal to no one but the people and frees me from any favoritism or obligation to any other interest than that of the public interest."(3e) Surprisingly, Johnson finished a strong third in the primary. He trailed Lowden by only 680 votes and Wood by 5,000. The New Republic reported that Johnson had "gained steadily on the other two men, and secured an amazing proportion of the votes. If he can show anything like the same proportionate strength at the convention in June, Hiram Johnson will be the arbiter of the result."(18)

Following the South Dakota primary Johnson swung east into Michigan where he campaigned vigorously against the League and allied intervention into Russia. Johnson made a very impressive showing by winning with 45,000 votes over his strongest rival, General Wood and defeated both Herbert Hoover and Lowden by a margin of over 100,000 votes. Some of Johnson's strength came from his position against the Russian intervention. His arguments were particularly popular because a large number of troops in that action were from Michigan. As a result of Johnson's victory, the New York Sun reported that this "placed Senator Hiram Johnson as a serious contender for the Republican presidential nomination."(102)

After Michigan Johnson carried his stump campaign through Missouri, Nebraska, North Dakota, Minnesota, Indiana, New Jersey, New York, North Carolina, Ohio, and Pennsylvania. He won the Nebraska and Montana primaries in April. He narrowly lost to Wood in New Jersey. Following his victories in Nebraska and Montana, Johnson went on to win primaries in Oregon and North Carolina; and even though he had not entered Governor Lowden's home state of Illinois, he received over 72,000 write-in votes. He also received over 16,000 votes in Ohio, another state where he had not entered. In Indiana, with the help of George Norris, Johnson fell 6,000 votes short of upsetting General Wood and polled more votes than Lowden and Harding combined.

The California primary was held May 4, 1920. Johnson was doubtful of his chances in his home state because of Hoover's candidacy and the popularity of the League there. At one point during the campaign Johnson confessed his fear that California would become "the graveyard of [his] ambition."(1) He faced strong opposition from the Los Angeles Times and the Los Angeles Express. He told Lissner that Hoover had the backing of big business and is "believed by our people to be a saint before whose shrine all must bow."(1) Nevertheless, after the ballots had been counted Johnson was declared the winner with 160,000 more votes than Hoover. In all, he received 370,819 votes.

Johnson's tremendous popularity was surprising to many political experts who had expected him to be eliminated early in the campaign. According to the New Republic, one of the reasons given for his victory was that the Republican bosses were really backing Johnson in order to eliminate Wood.(93) Other experts reevaluated the country's sentiment toward the League of Nations, which, based on Johnson's success, seemed to be drifting in the direction of his position.

An analysis of the primaries showed that Johnson received a total of 1,010,176 votes compared to 697,513 for

Wood, his closest rival. Lowden received 34,477, Hoover 298,778, and Harding 144,762. Years later, Harold Ickes wrote in his autobiography that, "Before Johnson was through he had won more votes in the strong Republican states than any rival. Had rules of fair play instead of the law of the jungle obtained, Hiram Johnson would have been nominated and elected."(11) Unfortunately, despite Johnson's overwhelming success before the populace, he entered the national convention with only 112 pledged delegates, 381 short of what was needed to win the nomination.

In early June, Johnson arrived in Chicago for the Republican convention. Several thousand supporters greeted him at the railway station. Then, accompanied by a brass band, Johnson marched along with his supporters to the Auditorium Hotel. No one could mistake the historical significance of the event. Johnson was following the same route and repeating the same things that Roosevelt had done in 1912. He even addressed the crowd from the window of his hotel room just as TR had done. The New York Times noted the similarity and speculated on the importance and meaning of Johnson's tactic. Rumors increased as to whether Johnson planned to bolt the party if not nominated.

On June 7, 1920, before a crowd at the Auditorium Theatre, scene of the Progressive bolt in 1912, Johnson attacked political bossism:

> These few, and the members of the press acting with them, are our real enemies. I deny their right to draw the line in the Republican Party against just common folks. These common folks made the party in its early beginning. They gave their blood that the nation might be saved for you and for me. . . . All its traditions, its marvelous history, the great galaxy of its immortals, its glorious past achievements, its present greatness, its future destiny, all cry out against the attempt made by a few today to dehumanize the Republican Party.(3e)

As the convention opened it became quite clear that the party bosses did not intend to allow Johnson to control the proceedings or to win the nomination. There were several delegates being contested, and out of the 137 Johnson received only seven.

Johnson's second major setback was the selection of the convention chairman. His forces favored William E. Borah. Henry Cabot Lodge was selected instead. Lodge was a party regular and not a Johnson supporter. Another major setback came during the speech nominating Johnson. He had selected Charles Stetson Wheeler from California to give the nominating speech, but Wheeler was a total failure. According to Oswald Villard, a writer for Nation, Wheeler "succeeded only in driving delegates away," and that "every moment he spoke made matters worse for the Californian for whom he appealed, so the Johnson candidacy collapsed in sad fashion."(136)   Other sources reported that Wheeler alienated many present by referring to delegates from the South as "hand-picked," and delegates from northern states as "political slaves" who need to "scourge" the political bosses from the party.(3e)

No one was able to command enough votes to win the nomination during the early balloting.   Johnson's hopes peaked on the third ballot, still 344 votes short of what he needed.   For all intents and purposes, Johnson had been eliminated as a presidential contender.   But he still controlled a large number of delegates and, therefore, received four different invitations to become the vice presidential nominee.   The offers came from Lowden, Wood, Knox, and Harding.   According to Johnson's son, the offer for Knox came from Boies Penrose of Philadelphia, one of the party bosses, who assured Johnson that "Knox was a very sick man."(1)   Johnson refused all of their offers.

Johnson's candidacy and campaign were badly handled from beginning to end. Villard observed that Johnson acted as if he were a total "novice in politics."   He had worked out no strategy for the convention and had not even appointed a floor manager to canvass the delegates for him or to work toward his nomination.(136)   The only major victory that Johnson could claim was a plank in the party platform denouncing the League of Nations.

Johnson left the convention a defeated man.   When asked to comment on Harding's nomination, he refused.   It was a day later before he sent a telegram congratulating Harding on his victory.(112)   A week later, Johnson declared to the press: "I am going to my home in California . . . to sit on the porch and look at the bay.   I have cleared my mind of politics completely.   Maybe after I have sat there for a while, I will make a statement."(3e)   During the next several weeks Johnson thought hard about his defeat, searching for reasons. To Meyer Lissner he confessed that: "You probably are entirely right . . . concerning my indulgence in sarcasm. This is a fault I own. . . .   Some of the newspapers in the East described me as entirely too emotional to be President. I think there was more or less justice in their criticism."(1)

Others, such as President-elect Harding, told Johnson that his major difficulty was his "indifference to party regularity" and that if he were to change there was nothing to prevent him from obtaining the nomination.(1)   The New York Times sympathetically reported that:   "Out in California a strong man sits broken hearted beside the sad sea waves. . . . Hiram Johnson left the Chicago convention profoundly dejected."

Johnson did not sit alone for long before party leaders

began pleading with him to campaign for Harding.   In October Johnson toured the Midwest and East in support of Harding.(3b)   The tour was by all accounts a total success. Senator Harry New, director of the party speakers' bureau, commented, "of all the speakers, Senator Johnson is easily the headliner.   He has got them all backed off the boards."(3e)   Johnson accepted the challenge of President Wilson and declared to his audiences, "this election is going to be the solemn referendum that [the president] wanted.   He is going to get it, and we are going to bury the League beyond all redemption."(3e)   Following the election the president-elect met with the senator in order to thank him for his efforts.   In addition, he assured Johnson that he would never return the Versailles treaty to the Senate and that the League would "not be taken in skeleton form or otherwise in any new endeavor."(1)

While the 1920 election marked the end of the League, it also signalled the end of the progressive movement.   The movement had been disintegrating since 1916 and the loss of Roosevelt.   Disagreements over foreign policy issues provided the final impetus.   After the election Johnson commented to William Jennings Bryan: "Reaction is on.   Whether the old spirit of progressivism can be aroused . . . during our generation, seems to be doubtful."(10)

Throughout the 1920s Johnson made what might be called token efforts at reform but without the vigor and tenacity of the past.   He announced on January 9, 1921, for example, that he would propose a national presidential primary law.   A federal statute, Johnson argued, would prevent party bosses from usurping the public in favor of special interests. Publicly he declared:

Progressivism has not passed, certain Progressives have. . . . The limelight Progressives who are more interested in office than in policies have wanted their horrible past forgotten, and have endeavored to atone by out-regularing regularity. . . . We witness the assault all along the line upon the direct primary.(3e)

Despite the enthusiasm of his public announcements, Johnson was unable to maintain a sustained effort on its behalf. Although he offered public encouragement to those in the Senate fighting for a national primary, he did very little himself.   His measure died quietly in the Judiciary Committee without much notice by the senator from California.

Johnson's most enthusiastic efforts were in opposition to the nomination of David H. Blair for commissioner of the Internal Revenue Service and William Howard Taft to the Supreme Court.   Johnson opposed both men vehemently, more for personal reasons than any other.   Blair had been a delegate from North Carolina at the last Republican convention in Chicago, and, despite the fact that Johnson had won the North

Carolina primary, he voted for Lowden.(18)

Johnson opposed Taft because of what had happened in 1912. He personally considered Taft "a man devoid of learning, judicial temperament, and of principle." He told Raymond Robbins that he had to oppose Taft's nomination because to do otherwise would have been "false to the old Roosevelt fight, false to every principle in which I believe, false to myself, and false to my country."(10) Nonetheless, Johnson believed that both Blair and Taft would be approved. Privately he despised many of his Senate colleagues for their lack of integrity. Regarding the proceedings and in a tirade of hyperbole, Johnson complained to his sons that:

> We have now a Senate more subservient, more servile, and contemptibly sycophantic than the Senate has ever been during my residence here. . . . As I faced the members of the Finance Committee . . . I looked at Penrose, Smoot, and McCumber, and I really believe these three men would connive at murder, if necessary, to carry out a nefarious political scheme or a party program. . . . I could see Smoot sitting in a darkened inner sanctum, calmly decreeing the death of one he did not like, but always sending another to execute the decree. McCumber is a man utterly without principle, and Penrose is best described as unmoral. My eyes passed from these three to the two New England members, Dillingham and McLean, both cold-nosed Yankees, each rich and thoroughly respectable, but each the mere tool of big interests, and honestly believing government to be an instrument for pillage by rapacious and dishonest business. . . . I passed then along to Jim Watson of Indiana. He would never murder. He is too cowardly for that, but if your back were turned, and he had the opportunity, without discovery, to drop poison in your food or your water, he would do it, and then be the first one to commiserate with you in your pain and torture. These are the fellows who are trying the Blair case.(1)

Johnson's failure in 1920 to win the Republican presidential nomination led to disillusionment, despair and desperation. He blamed others for his failure, and he considered those who opposed him to be despicable men conspiring against the nation. He was also plagued by the defection of former friends and supporters. Unable to perceive any weakness in his own personality or beliefs, Johnson was inclined to believe that their previous support was in reality only a guise in order to gain political favor and power. His personal letters and comments reflected an intolerance toward those who opposed him. In contrast, he perceived himself to be the champion of the people, struggling against injustice, deceit, and dishonesty.

This conviction was further reinforced by his failure to prevent the ratification of the Four Powers Pact between the

United States, Great Britain, France, and Japan in 1921 and 1922. He was convinced that the Four Powers Pact was nothing more than another attempt by England to force the United States into a subordinate role and that those supporting it in the Senate were merely using another tactic to involve this country in the League of Nations. Its ratification was evidence to Johnson that his enemies were successfully closing in on him.(5)

His final defeat was inevitable, Johnson believed, and would come in 1922 when he was up for reelection. Nonetheless, he refused to surrender without a fight, declaring publicly that he intended to seek another term. Johnson remembered the 1922 senatorial race as one of his hardest fought campaigns. In the primaries he was opposed by Charles C. Moore, a wealthy farmer from southern California. Although relatively unknown when compared to the national reputation of Johnson, Moore was supported by a host of newspapers, including Chester Rowell's Fresno Republican. This was an unfortunate blow to Johnson because Rowell had long been one of his closest friends and most ardent supporters. Johnson was also opposed by Harry Chandler and the Los Angeles Times, Edward Dickson of the Los Angeles Express, and F. W. Kellogg with a string of over thirteen papers.(112)

However, Johnson still enjoyed the support of C. K. McClatchy with his Sacramento paper and William Randolph Hearst with his newspaper empire. A critical issue during the campaign was the Fordney-McCumber tariff, which was still pending in the Senate. Johnson supported the tariff which was exactly what any politician wishing votes in California should have done. According to the New York Times, "having befriended 117 crops, Johnson is fortified in all parts of the state."

During the election one issue of interest to many of the voters in the state was the Boulder Canyon project, a bill then pending in Congress which proposed the building of a dam in the Boulder Canyon region. According to the governmental Reclamation Service the dam would significantly increase the supply of water available in Nevada, Arizona, and California, making possible the development and reclamation of over a million acres. It would also provide a significant amount of electricity for municipalities in southern California and would solve the flood problems created by the Colorado River. Johnson, who was cosponsoring the bill with Congressman Phil Swing, had just introduced the bill into the Senate.

Characteristically, Johnson relied on a stump campaign as his primary strategy, opening at the Los Angeles Philharmonic Auditorium in July. According to the San Francisco Chronicle over 8,500 enthusiastic supporters packed the house, and many more were forced to stand in the street because of a lack of room. Johnson wasted no time in attacking his opponents.   Early in the speech he declared:

> Blatant in their indecency, flagrant in their audacity
> for every existing wrong, ruthless in their mendacity
> against every man and woman seeking reform, denouncing,
> abusing, reviling the good people of the State who were
> determined to have not only a moral but a just
> commonwealth, ever stood HARRY CHANDLER and the "LOS
> ANGELES TIMES," and with them were those whom they could
> cajole or frighten; the timid and the weak, the vicious
> and the wicked, whom they ever drove this way and that,
> with the threat of newspaper ridicule and abuse.(1)

Johnson recognized that his stand regarding foreign
policy threatened to alienate many of his former supporters.
To this, he argued, "In the multiplicity of matters which
come before the Senate it often happens that the allies of
today are the antagonists of tomorrow." In justification of
his vote against the Four Powers Pact he declared:

> I conceive the duty of a public official to give all that
> is in him to those he represents. He can do this only
> with his best judgment and following his conscience. If
> he is the mere weather vane of transient public clamor,
> he merits no man's respect, and worse still, he loses his
> own.   While I am in public office, I shall ever do as I
> have done in the past, act according to the light God
> gives me.   I never was and I never will be a mere rubber
> stamp to register the will of any man or any set of men.
> While I was Governor ever before my eyes upon the wall of
> the Governor's office, now before me in my office in the
> national Capitol, are these framed words of Abraham
> Lincoln:
>> "I am not bound to win, but I am bound to be true.
>> I am not bound to succeed, but I am bound to live up
>> to what light I have.   I must stand with anybody
>> that stands right; stand with him while he is right,
>> and part with him when he goes wrong."
> By this rule, I measure my public acts.(1)

According to newspaper accountes, Johnson's stump
campaign was successful.   In the southern part of the state
his audiences were described as enthusiastic and supportive.
The Sacramento Bee, McClatchy's paper, reported that during a
single day's campaigning Johnson spoke to as many as 10,000
people, receiving cheers and "fine ovations" wherever he
appeared.

Despite the reports of enthusiastic audiences, Johnson's
prospects were still in doubt.   Opposition newspapers
referred to various polls showing a fifty-fifty split in San
Francisco, and a two-to-one lead for Moore over Johnson in
Los Angeles.   According to Ralph Arnold, one of Moore's major
supporters, the San Joaquin and Sacramento valleys were
responding to Moore's candidacy much more favorably than they

had expected.(112)   The New York Times predicted that, "the defeat of Senator Hiram Johnson looms as a probability in the Republican primary of tomorrow."

However, the results surprised Moore and shocked his supporters. Johnson defeated Moore by more than 75,000 votes and in the general election he defeated his Democratic opponent, William Pearson, handily by a much greater margin than he had his opponent in 1916. Johnson had been vindicated by the voters. Even the New York Times declared that, "Johnson was opposed by the most powerful forces that ever have sought to tear down the ideals of popular government for which Hiram Johnson has fought. It was a great and deserved triumph."

Johnson's popularity helped to keep alive his hopes to win the presidential nomination in 1924 or 1928. His overwhelming victory meant that he had not been removed from the path of Herbert Hoover, who was also preparing for a bid for the presidency. During the senatorial campaign, Arnold had concluded that, "if we don't lick Johnson, we have little chance of ever doing anything for Hoover in the bigger things we have in mind."(112)

Hoover and Johnson were not the only men in 1922 planning for the presidential race two years hence. Robert La Follette was also in the running. In December, 1922, La Follette called a meeting in Washington to discuss the possibility of nominating a Progressive at the 1924 Republican convention, or the possibility of reorganizing a third party. Johnson, viewing it merely as a strategy by La Follette to gain support for his own candidacy, refused to attend. Johnson wrote to his eldest son that, "La Follette has seized his opportunity and has organized what Roosevelt used to term the 'lunatic fringe' composed of all the crazy advocates of 'isms' there are in the country."(1) Johnson's political enemies, however, did not allow his absence to go unnoticed. He was assailed by several newspapers for his refusal to attend and accused of deserting the progressive cause.

The future plans of none of these men, La Follette, Hoover, or Johnson, had much chance of success if Harding were to decide to seek a second term which, at the time, seemed very likely. Johnson was convinced that neither La Follette or himself could effectively challenge the president for the nomination. He told Raymond Robbins that "if Harding wants to be re-nominated, there is nothing that can prevent it. The system is such, and the power of the office such that he can obtain a majority of delegates in a convention."(1)

With Harding's nomination a foregone conclusion, Johnson turned his attention toward other matters of interest. In particular, Johnson prepared for the upcoming fight against entry into the World Court, which he viewed as another attempt to involve the United States with the League of Nations.  He laid the groundwork for his arguments against the World Court with an article titled, "Why 'Irreconcilables' Keep Out of Europe," published in the New York Times, January 14, 1923, and inserted into the Congressional Record two days later.(213)  His article was significant because it established him as the sole remaining leader of those senators against American involvement in European affairs.  He complained to his son in January, 1923, that he was the only irreconcilable of any stature still fighting to prevent America's entrance into the League of Nations.(1)

President Harding's death on August 2, 1923 threw the Republican party into chaos and created a void in leadership.  Johnson, as well as others, could now declare their candidacy without seeming disloyal to the party.  In analyzing this new development, the New York Times noted that "Johnson is now in a position to . . . call upon those Senators of the old guard who have been manifesting a friendly disposition toward him, to show their good faith by giving him their support for the nomination."  Johnson wasted no time in establishing his interest in running.  In early September, just a few weeks after Harding's death, he wrote to Harold Ickes instructing him that he could go ahead and set up "paper committees in states like Illinois" in preparation for his presidential campaign.(1)

While Johnson was busy thinking about what issues would highlight his campaign, Coolidge was seeking the support from conservative elements, and unfortunately for Johnson, many of the old guard, such as George Moses from New Hampshire, found new hope for victory in the new president.  Harold Ickes complained that "most senators willing to overthrow Harding, were unwilling to be irregular under Coolidge."(11)

Johnson also found many Progressives against him.  His fight against the proposed international conference to discuss disarmament brought him the opposition of Senator Borah of Idaho and Kenyon of Iowa, both of whom had supported his candidacy in 1920.  Senator Magnus Johnson, from Wisconsin, declared, "I used to be for Hiram . . . but he has backslid."(130)  Many of these men switched their allegiance to La Follette who appeared to be a much more progressive candidate and who also offered a much less radical position regarding foreign policy issues.

Nonetheless, Johnson was determined to run for the presidency.  He officially announced his candidacy on November 15, 1923, in Chicago, declaring that there were two philosophies within the Republican party.  One was "ultra-conservative, materialistic, stolidly and stubbornly resisting any change and vigorously contesting every human advance."  The other, which he supported, was "mindful of existing rights, but recognizing conditions and mankind's gradual process, is idealistic and forward looking."(18)

Johnson hardly mentioned Coolidge and ignored La Follette completely. The New Republic declared that he was "most inoffensive about his opponents as men. He merely questions their philosophy of government, he does not divulge what the antagonists are or how specifically they differ."(103) His only direct statement was his reassurance that he was strongly against any type of American involvement, directly or indirectly with the League of Nations. This declaration set the tone of his campaign. Throughout the next few months he vigorously attacked his opponents on the issue of the World Court, almost completely ignoring critical domestic issues.

It was not until January before Johnson announced any type of political platform, and it was as vague as his earlier statements. His opposition to the World Court constituted the primary issue in his platform, while domestic issues played a secondary role. After reviewing it carefully, the Outlook, normally favorable toward Johnson, noted that his anti-League position "will have weight only with those who already agree with him."(99) Overall, his platform offered little popular appeal. He primarily voiced opposition to a variety of plans, while in substance he was vague, offering no specific proposals of his own. In short, he had no platform.

Without widespread support Johnson's campaign had little chance of success. He opened in Cleveland on January 3, 1924. Excerpts of the address carried by the Associated Press indicate that he emphasized foreign policy such as the recent transfer of arms to the Mexican government and declared:

> Our policy is that the United States frowns on revolutions . . . we, who were born in revolution . . . says to the people inhabiting the continent, "If you dare fight for what you deem to be right, if you raise your hand against oppression and wrong, the most powerful nation of the world will come to the aid of those you think your oppressors, and will maintain existing power. . . ."(1)

During the next few weeks Johnson travelled through Michigan, Indiana, and Illinois. Overall, he was dissatisfied with his campaign. He confessed to his sons: "It has been a terrible experience. I have been practically alone and have never utilized my vitality so harshly. I am so physically exhausted that I care little what happens."(1)

On April 8, 1923, primaries were held in Illinois and Nebraska. Johnson lost by large margins in both states. He also lost badly in Michigan and North Dakota a week later.

His only victory was in South Dakota, a state without many
delegates. For all intents and purposes, Johnson was
eliminated from the race. Unfortunately, he could not
withdraw his name from those states where he had already been
entered. He sadly wrote to his sons:

> Three primaries remain, New Jersey, Ohio, Indiana, in
> which good people have gone to bat for me and I cannot
> abandon and desert them if they want me to come into
> their state. Recent results of course make these trips
> useless, but the least I can do is to aid those who have
> helped me and I shall probably go into each state
> briefly.(1)

He was also entered in the California primary, but could not
bring himself to campaign in his home state for what was
obviously a lost cause. At the same time, he was unwilling
to admit total defeat. In a symbolic gesture of good will,
he sent a message to the voters of California declaring:

> No righteous cause is ever lost. "My head is bloody but
> unbowed," and still "I am the master of my fate, the
> captain of my soul." But though I make no personal
> appeal, because I was by circumstances such an intimate
> part of the accomplishment and achievement of California,
> because with you I led a great people from political
> bondage to political freedom and made a corrupt and
> subservient government truly responsive and
> representative and gave it back to those to whom it
> belonged, it is not only my right but my duty to appeal
> for those for whom I strove and for whom I wrought for
> the things we did and the proud position we obtained. I
> will survive any result of the primary and will go my way
> with courage unabated and spirit undoughted. . . . I
> leave the decision with you.(1)

Despite the eloquence of his emotional appeal,
Republican voters rejected Johnson in favor of Calvin
Coolidge. In all, Johnson received 262,499 votes while
Coolidge received 311,826. It was the only defeat at the
polls that Johnson ever experienced during his entire career
in California politics. In an effort to minimize the
significance of his loss Johnson, when asked to make a
statement, replied that, "many desired to register their
protest, if nothing more, and did so."(3e) Shortly following
the primary Johnson retreated to Washington, D.C., refusing
to endorse any other candidate. In addition, he did not
attend the Republican convention and rejected every request
soliciting his help during the upcoming general election.(1)

## Coolidge and Hoover: Lean Years for Johnson

With the defeats of Hiram Johnson in the 1924
presidential primaries and Robert La Follette in the general

election the nation appeared to be firmly locked in the grip
of conservativism.  As a result of the old guard's victory,
the sweeping reforms of the past decade became but dim
memories.  Laissez faire policies and "business as usual"
were the new cries.  Few Progressives were left in the Senate
to echo the cause of reform.  Those who survived the tidal
wave of political change found their ranks thinning because
of division, political attrition, and old age.  The great
midwestern liberal, La Follette, died of a heart attack in
1925, leaving Johnson as the only surviving Progressive who
had run for the presidency.  In addition to this loss, Albert
J. Beveridge, an old and close friend of Johnson's, died two
years later.  Following the death of Senator Ferris of
Michigan in March of 1928, Johnson lamented to his sons that
their deaths affected him greatly: "They come all in a bunch
now, in an ever increasing list.  The thought of it dampens
the ardor of our little struggles, and neither our little
triumphs nor our little defeats seem of great
consequence."(1)

Johnson's greatest desolation was not the loss of old
colleagues and friends, however, but rather his continued
dissatisfaction with his party.  Johnson became one of the
greatest vocal antagonists to the administrations of both
Presidents Coolidge and Hoover.  Like a lone wolf hunting his
prey, Johnson stalked the Senate chambers awaiting
opportunities to attack his political enemies, taking a
certain pride in his political solitude, viewing it as a
demonstration of his intellectual superiority and personal
integrity over others whom considered too corrupt or too
timid to speak out against party bosses.  After one speech
Johnson bragged that "two hard-boiled Republican senators,
who are for the measure, tell me, with very great emotion,
how they approved of everything I said, and how they longed
to do as I was doing, but did not dare.  This is a terrible
thing in a Republic."(1)  Even in the face of defeat, Johnson
remained a formidable and dangerous foe.  The mere rumor that
he intended to speak filled the galleries and his popularity
allowed Johnson to influence major legislation.

During the 1920s and 1930s Johnson concentrated on
foreign affairs.  By 1926 the question of whether the United
States would adhere to decisions made by the World Court had
still not been resolved.  Ever since its introduction in
1923, Johnson remained its greatest opponent.  Why, he asked,
should Americans "submit ourselves to the determination of
Europe."(1)  Acceptance of the court, in Johnson's view, was
the first step toward eventual involvement in the League of
Nations.

During World War I four liberty loans were raised in the
United States.  These loans in combination with victory
loans, raised to help with the reconstruction of Europe,
amounted to over nine and a half billion dollars, making the
United States the major creditor of European nations.

Following the end of the war and the advent of economic problems the collection of repayments became increasing difficult, creating a major controversy. Some believed that the United States should cancel these debts, while others such as Johnson bitterly opposed cancellation. The proponents argued that repayment placed an enormous economic burden on Europe, a burden that they argued would cause economic disaster. In contrast Johnson pointed to the increasing number of foreclosures in this country. At the same time, he argued, European countries were increasing their spending on armaments while they continued to claim that they could not afford to repay the loans. Yet, Johnson argued, "the very men who have thus so generously scattered our money all over Europe, cynically and contemptuously say, we must not devote a very small fraction of the amount to the endeavor to aid those who are suffering in our own land."(277)

Most of the nations in Europe defaulted within the next few years. Only Finland completely paid off its debt; Italy offered token payments, but on the whole, the loans were never repaid. Related to this question was the World Court controversy which Johnson feared might make judgments on war debts. It would be ridiculous, Johnson argued, that "the creditor nations of the earth should be put at the mercy of their debtors."(1) Although Johnson's argument was appealing, the Senate nonetheless passed a motion favoring U.S. adherence to the decisions of the World Court. The Senate also passed a reservation forbidding the Court from entertaining any request for a decision on a question of interest to the United States without its consent. The other powers, as one might have expected, found the reservation unacceptable. So, for all effective purposes, the move to join the World Court was prevented by Johnson and his colleagues through the reservation.

President Hoover failed again in 1929 to win Senate approval of the Court without reservations. The issue remained dormant until President Franklin Roosevelt revived it during his administration. Johnson voiced his opposition and found support from William Randolph Hearst, Will Rogers, and the well-known radio priest, Charles Coughlin. Once again the proponents failed to obtain the needed two-thirds majority. Following this fight, Johnson remarked to his son that the World Court issue had been "the toughest, and the biggest and most far-reaching contest legislatively in which ever I have been engaged."(1)

The World Court issue provides a key to understanding Johnson's view regarding the relationship between foreign affairs and progressivism. Unlike many of his former colleagues who saw his anti-internationalism as a repudiation of progressive principles, Johnson saw it as consistent rather than antithetical. He feared that any involvement in international organizations might threaten the advancement of reform and viewed every attempt to establish ties with European countries as a conspiracy by international bankers to bilk hugh profits from the American taxpayer in order to finance foreign intrigues. Thus Johnson saw himself as the defender of progressivism rather than its adversary.

During the 1920s Johnson opposed almost every form of international involvement. He voted against the League of Nations, the World Court, the Four Powers Pact, the Reparations Commission, the London Naval Treaty, and the moratorium on war debts. Ironically, he was only successful in preventing American involvement in what many thought were the two most significant institutions, the League of Nations and the World Court.

Johnson broke faith with his principles on only two occasions, on the Nine Powers Pact and the Kellogg-Briand Anti-War Treaty. The Nine Powers Pact respected the sovereignty, independence, and integrity of China and pledged to maintain the Open Door Policy. In principle Johnson agreed with this but opposed the provision that the powers should meet for "full and frank discussions" when a violation of the treaty occurred. This provision, he felt, obligated the United States to involve itself in a dispute if the majority of nations voted for action. Nevertheless, Johnson voted in favor of the motion arguing that, "I vote for the ratification . . . only because it modifies and minimizes the four-power treaty. I would not vote for it if it were given an independent instrument; but I vote for it solely and alone because it modifies the other treaty.(18)

Johnson voted for the Kellogg-Briand Anti-War Treaty for different reasons. Basically, the treaty, formulated and proposed by the French Foreign Minister Aristide Briand and Secretary of State Kellogg, renounced war as an instrument of foreign policy. Johnson called it the "Kellogg Piffle Pact," proclaiming that in reality it was of "no consequence." Speaking just prior to the vote on the Kellogg-Briand Pact, he reported that his vote in favor of the treaty was based on the slim hope that it might lead to peace. Johnson also quoted to his colleagues a verse from Justin McCarthy's "If I were King" to demonstrate the folly of their hopes:

To Messire [sic] Noel, named the neat/ By those who love him, I bequeath/ A helmless ship, a houseless street/ A wordless book, a swordless sheath/ A hourless clock, a leafless wreath/ A bed sans sheet, a board sans meat/ A bell sans tongue, a saw sans teeth/ To make his nothingless complete(286)

Throughout his career Johnson voiced skepticism toward all forms of international agreements, viewing them as extensions of Europe's greed, power, and hunger for conquest. These international documents were not negotiated for humanitarian purposes or to ensure peace as their proponents claimed, but rather, according to Johnson, to consolidate their power and increase their empires. Johnson's voicing of these doubts caused the press and his political enemies to call him an isolationist, a term he resented:

> When you call us in derision "isolationists" you do not know what you say. Isolationists? Not a bit of it. I would not be isolated from the rest of the world, of course, in any of those contacts which for 140 years we have always had. I would not be isolated from the rest of the world in those contacts with which we have all become familiar during the period we have been a Nation. But Mr. President, I would keep this country from Europe's politics, from Europe's wars, from Europe's agreements, which European statesmen seem to think make us a part of their collection agencies and make us a part of their political policies that have created the awful maelstrom over there.(275)

Johnson fully admitted that the United States was a major exporter and that a large portion of the economy depended on involvement in overseas commerce. In lieu of international treaties Johnson was a vigorous advocate for a strong navy and defense. This position was based primarily on the assumption that the United States was not popular. As he repeatedly reminded his Senate colleagues, "there is scarcely among the nations of the earth a single one but regards us with hostility and ill will, and in many cases downright hatred." Sarcastically, he quoted the mayor of Beverly Hills: "The only way we could get in worse would be to help them win another war." In Johnson's view, the nation's only guarantee of protection against its "loyal allies" was a strong defense. Rhetorically, he asked, ". . . shall we, disliked by all, stand naked and defenseless?" As an avid supporter of sea power Johnson argued:

> The Monroe Doctrine is just as strong as the United States Navy, and no stronger. Our foreign policy rests for its foundation not upon our will, but upon our ability to defend that will. We have, with a generosity unparalleled in history, yielded the power that was ours, and have accepted a situation equal to that of others when we were far beyond them, with the possibility of outstripping all the nations of the earth combined. We have been more than just to Great Britain and Japan. What I ask, sir, is that there should be some justice to America now.(280)

Johnson saw the growing menace of Japanese naval power and argued for a strong navy to counteract it. This issue and others of similar nature Johnson found to be the most fascinating and critical problems facing the nation. As a result they absorbed an increasing amount of Johnson's time in the Senate.

Johnson was also concerned with many domestic problems. He sponsored legislation in the Senate proposing medical care and education for American Indians, compensation for disabled seamen and veterans, protection and conservation of national forests, and new immigration laws. He spoke in favor of proposals for unemployment insurance, a minimum wage, protection of labor's right to strike, and investigation of the granting of federal oil leases.

In addition, Johnson favored relief for farmers. Since the end of World War I the economic plight of American farmers had been a major problem. An increasing number were laden with enormous debt; and because of low and uncertain prices for crops many were threatened with foreclosure. In May, 1929, after years of unsuccessful attempts to find support for a satisfactory solution, Johnson pleaded with his colleagues: "If there is ever an obligation upon those who pretend to serve a great people, that obligation rests upon both sides of this Chamber, upon Republicans, upon Democrats, and Republican-Democrats, in this body and elsewhere."(18) Unfortunately, Johnson's plea for nonpartisanship fell upon deaf ears. Like most of the progressive legislation proposed in Congress during the 1920s, it died quietly in committee.

Other than the Boulder Dam project, the only efforts by Johnson in the Senate concerning domestic problems with which he experienced some measure of success were those on behalf of the coal miners in West Virginia and Pennsylvania. In 1923 Johnson sponsored a resolution demanding an investigation of conditions at the coal mines. The resolution passed but accomplished little else. By 1928 the conditions had worsened causing widespread strikes. The owners responded with lockouts and the closing of many mines, thus creating more poverty and hatred among the workers. Moved by coal-miner's desperate pleas for help, Johnson fought vigorously on their behalf.

Armed with reports sent to him from unbiased observers as well as newspaper articles which he obtained himself, Johnson presented one of his most impassioned pleas in the Senate. He presented his speech February 1, 1928, just three weeks after he had introduced a resolution requesting an investigation.

During the speech Johnson narrated a collection of eye witness accounts describing the conditions at the mines and the subsequent actions by the mine owners to repress the striking workers. By the time he reached his conclusion Johnson had quoted stories from four different reporters writing in five different newspapers; a petition from thirty-five clergymen from almost every conceivable denomination; a horror story from a single Baptist preacher; an account by a social worker; testimony from the former governor of Pennsylvania, Gifford Pinchot; testimony from the chairman of a presidential investigating committee; and a court case prohibiting miners from attending church. In addition to the specific accounts, Johnson offered another 218 affidavits attesting to the illegal actions and violence committed by representatives of the mine owners. Johnson passionately ended his speech, declaring:

> I plead no cause of theirs. They need no such feeble voice as mine. I do plead, sir, another cause; I do plead the cause of women who are weak, of mothers who have not the milk for their babes, of babes who come into the world in shacks where the wind blows and howls, and snow comes in upon the suffering mother and newborn babe. I plead for this investigation, and I ask it for this one reason alone--I plead for it because of humanity. Humanity demands it!(283)

The resolution passed the Senate unanimously without the need for a roll call vote.

Following his plea for the miners Johnson turned his attention toward his own welfare. In 1928 his term in the Senate was ending and he had to begin working for reelection. By this time the Hoover forces had gained in strength and were making their move for the Republican presidential nomination. Johnson personally disliked Hoover and viewed him as a mere opportunist who was devoid of all morals and lacking in integrity.(1) In 1928, however, the expediency of self interest dictated that he not follow his instincts.

Hoover was in the same position. He wanted to win the nomination; and with Johnson opposing his candidacy his chances might be greatly diminished. Likewise, Johnson did not want the Hoover forces rallied against him while he sought reelection. It was therefore in the interests of both men not to campaign against each other. So, a temporary truce, negotiated by Bert Meek, one of Johnson's lieutenants, was honored by both parties. Without opposition from the Hoover forces Johnson was easily elected to a third Senate term.(1)

As soon as the election was over Johnson once again became one of Hoover's strongest political enemies, opposing him on every piece of major legislation. He vehemently opposed Hoover when he called for a moratorium on the collection of war debts and when he proposed adherence to the World Court. Following the stock market crash in October, 1929, Johnson attacked Hoover's domestic policies. He presented scathing denunciations against Hoover for proposing to spend millions of dollars to help business while at the same time proposing nothing to help the millions who were unemployed. He told Ickes that "apparently no crisis finds the Great Engineer prepared, and when difficulties arise, he hastens to blunder."(1) He declared to others that "the best thing that could happen to the Republican Party would be to have Mr. Hoover retire."(1)

By 1931 there was widespread dissatisfaction with Hoover and his handling of the depression. Many Republicans such as Harold Ickes, who saw the economic crisis as a rare opportunity to defeat the old guard and revitalize the progressive movement, believed that Johnson might be able to win the presidential election. By mid-year Ickes was joined in his support of Johnson by Robert R. McCormick, owner of the Chicago Tribune; Senators Bronson Cutting, Smith W. Brookhart, Gerald Nye, Charles McNary, and Governor Gifford Pinchot. Ickes reported that $200,000 had been raised in campaign funds.(10)

Although flattered by the support, Johnson refused to become a candidate. He wrote his son that "while I think that my decision was wise, the gambler and adventurer in me make me regret that I am not making an ass of myself and running about the country."(1) Nevertheless, Johnson enjoyed "worrying the old man in the White House" and took a certain satisfaction in the fact that Hoover did not enter the primaries in North Dakota and Illinois partly because of a fear that Johnson intended to challenge him.(1)

## FDR, The New Deal, and Neutrality: The Final Years

During the first few months of 1932, following his decision not to enter the presidential race, Johnson was publicly silent regarding the political situation. Privately, he advised many of his close friends not to support Hoover. He told C. K. McClatchy, "I have in my mind the fixed idea that Hoover looks forward to a dictatorship, if not before the election, at least, if he is successful again, after the election."(1)

Hoover had a good chance for reelection, Johnson wrote, because "every predatory interest in the country is behind Hoover, and surreptitiously, the so-called power trust, will spend unlimited sums to elect Hoover and defeat Roosevelt."(1) Johnson liked Roosevelt, but feared that his position in the Republican Party might be destroyed by a public endorsement. On the other hand, Johnson could not fathom the thought of Hoover's reelection. Johnson's belief that Hoover was backed by Wall Street eventually propelled him into the Roosevelt camp. Johnson told his sons that "the one thing that draws to Roosevelt those of us who believe in real democracy is the character of the opposition to him. This opposition embraces all of those who believe in the right to exploit government for their own selfish advantage."(1)

A visit to Johnson's home in early July by John Sanford Cohen, vice-chairman of the Democratic National Committee, along with other leading Democrats, helped to fuel rumors that Johnson would announce his support of Roosevelt.(3e) Johnson, however, kept the press waiting. He neither denied nor confirmed the allegations. Through September Johnson vigorously attacked Hoover and the federal government's economic policy:

> Unemployment has increased and wages have decreased. Banks have been given money with a generosity never before exercised. Has this money reached those who, upon fair, ordinary, security, seek loans? Railroads have received the funds of the government which belongs to all. Have railroads maintained their wages? Banks haven't resumed normal lending and railroads have reduced the wages of their employees.(18)

While Johnson was speaking in Modesto, California, to the Federation of Labor, Roosevelt spoke from a railroad car in Sacramento, less than forty miles away. Using some notes provided by Raymond Moley, one of his advisers, FDR praised Johnson and referred to him, "as a man who had done so much to further progressive thought and courageous public action. . . . a warrior in the ranks of true American progress."(3e) Roosevelt continued to court Senator Johnson and his followers throughout his entire California tour by aligning himself with the liberal philosophy of the Progressives.(178) Johnson was impressed by Roosevelt's remarks and convinced that they had similar political philosophies. Johnson told some of his senatorial colleagues that FDR received "pretty general approval, and his very pleasing personality was quite attractive."(10)

In October, Johnson received a telegram from E. P. Clark and the representatives of over seventy California newspapers demanding that he announce his support for the Republican candidate.(3e) Feeling that he could no longer remain uncommitted, he publicly announced his decision. Johnson declared to the press that there were two philosophies of government. He supported the progressive. Hoover supported the ultra-conservative. As a "stand-patter" Hoover only paid lip service to what Johnson called "common humanity." Hoover courted special interests and by "his indifference" allowed the "ruthless exploitation of our people" by the power trust through the sale of foreign securities to "trusting American investors." In announcing his position Johnson boldly proclaimed:

> In this crisis I stress loyalty to the American people. . . . I was elected by men and women of all shades of political opinion, Democrats, Progressive, and conservative Republicans,--by the people of the State of California. I would not taint my record nor stultify myself now by abandoning the principles for which I have battled unceasingly during my career. The Republican Party is not at stake in this campaign. It is only the ambition of one man. . . . In the present cataclysm,

with eleven million unemployed, and suffering and want on
every hand, the man who puts his party fealty and his
hope of political preferment above the welfare of our
people does the worst possible disservice to his
country. . . .    I cannot and will not support
Mr. Hoover.(3e)

The Democrats were delighted by Johnson's statement.
Roosevelt's campaign manager, James A. Farley, described
Johnson's announcement as "one of the finest definitions of
progressivism" and predicted Hoover's defeat in November.(18)

In late October Johnson announced that he would stump
California and part of the Midwest on Roosevelt's behalf.
His first speech was given in San Francisco, October 28,
1932.    He also spoke in Los Angeles, Chicago, and Rockford,
Illinois.    Both the San Francisco and Chicago addresses were
broadcast nationally.    His live audiences ranged between
8,000 and 10,000.(18)    He described Hoover's administration
as "inept . . . ineffective, inefficient, disastrous,
. . . un-American. . ." and concluded:

The crisis demands a change.
    When a miracle man fails and a mystery man explodes,
instinctively we turn to one who knows and understands
and feels with us.    In this campaign such a man is
Franklin Roosevelt.    He is no miracle or mystery man.    He
is just an American.(3e)

In the final tally, Roosevelt carried California by a margin
of over 475,000 votes.    Roosevelt was appreciative of
Johnson's efforts and shortly after the election asked
Johnson to become secretary of the interior.    Johnson thanked
the new president for his confidence but told him that he
preferred to remain in the Senate.(1)    Johnson confided to
his close friend, McClatchy:

I do not want any position with it.    The Lord, I fear,
made me a natural rebel, or as I would prefer to phrase
it, with a passionate independence. . . .    I would rather
cease political life than sacrifice the absolute freedom
of action politically in behalf of governmental policies
I have exercised.(1)

Initially, Johnson was one of Roosevelt's most ardent
supporters in the Senate.    He voted "yes" on practically all
of Roosevelt's New Deal measures, such as the 10 percent
increase in the tax of higher bracket incomes, the bill
creating the Securities & Exchange Commission and regulation
of the sale of stocks and bonds, the bill to provide a
retirement system for railway employees, the Agricultural
Adjustment Act, the Wagner Labor Act, the holding company
bill, the banking bill, the Soil Conservation Act, the bill
to provide funds for work relief, and the Social Security
Act.    Johnson told one of his friends:

We are taking many shots in the dark and much that
Roosevelt is doing may turn out to be of no value, but how
infinitely better it is to have a man of this sort at the
head of the game now than to have one who cries and whines
and talks of hair shirts and the awful burden that rests
upon him.(10)

To the press Johnson referred to Roosevelt as "a bold
and gallant gentleman with the adventure of youth and the
wisdom of age."(18)    Similarly, Roosevelt seemed to like
Johnson.    Johnson and his wife were often invited to dine at
the White House, and the senator sometimes lunched with the
president.    While they ate, Johnson advised the president on
various bills pending in the Senate and on possible
tactics.(1)  Although the two men appeared to like each other
and to have similar political philosophies, Roosevelt was
much more of an internationalist than Johnson.

Roosevelt's and Johnson's first major confrontation came
when Congress convened in January, 1934.  During the previous
session, the Senate had debated a bill proposed by Johnson to
protect American investors from fraudulent foreign
securities.  On February 2, 1934, the Johnson Act came up in
the Senate for a vote .  The act banned the floating of war
debts and prevented the president from declaring token
payments by European nations as sufficient to meet their
obligations.

Roosevelt was not in favor of the bill, but remained
relatively silent because of public sentiment.  Through the
help of some of his supporters in the Senate Roosevelt
managed to eliminate provisions in the act controlling
private loans.  The Johnson Act finally passed the Congress
in April.  It was the first legislation passed following
World War I limiting the president's power in foreign affairs
and was a prelude to the neutrality acts passed between 1935
and 1937.  The Johnson Act was important because it was the
high point of the senator's long fight to prevent American
involvement in European affairs.

In 1934, despite their disagreement over foreign policy,
Johnson received "Roosevelt's benediction"(18)   and was
nominated to succeed himself by the Republican, Democratic,
Prohibitionist, and Progressive parties.  His only opposition
in the general election came from a candidate nominated by
the Socialist Party.  Johnson easily won reelection in
November.

Johnson was not the only Roosevelt-backed candidate to
win in 1934.  Following the election, the Congress appeared
to be made up almost entirely of pro-Roosevelt men.  Johnson
saw this new development as dangerous.  He told his youngest
son:

> The "yes" men and the "rubber stamps" have been so multiplied by the election that there will be little independence in the forthcoming session, which means little real consideration of the legislation proposed by the Administration. It needs no argument to demonstrate that this is an evil thing in democracy.(1)

These developments would result, Johnson believed, in Roosevelt desiring an increasing role by the United States in international affairs.

FDR's and Johnson's second confrontation came over the World Court issue. Johnson admitted that up until an hour before the vote he feared that the administration might win. In anticipation, he had reserved some time just before the vote in order to "denounce in unmeasured terms the pressure and the bludgeoning that had gone on . . . and the attitude of some of our 'best people.'" But after he was able to come to an "understanding with our standpat Republicans" and was assured that they would support him, he switched the text of his address and devoted his time to the "Forgotten Men of American History."(314)  Following the vote, Arthur Knock, writing in the New York Times, proclaimed that Senator Johnson was "largely responsible for the outcome."  According to another source, the real fight occurred much earlier in the Foreign Relations Committee. Here too Johnson was given credit for swaying votes. As one "Administration senator described the scene, 'He made us stop, look and listen.'"

The World Court issue was important for two reasons. First, it shattered the illusion of Roosevelt's invincibility.  Second, it widened the growing rift between Johnson and the president. After Roosevelt's defeat on this issue Johnson received fewer invitations to the White House. Roosevelt's displeasure with Johnson did not immediately become apparent, however, because Roosevelt was too experienced a politician to risk alienating Johnson when he still wanted the senator's support in the upcoming election. And thus, he made overtures to Johnson in order to patch up their differences. In July Johnson was invited on the president's yacht for fishing and a short cruise, apparently as a gesture of good will.(1)  In spite of the president's charm and friendliness, Johnson remained uncommitted. Throughout the spring and summer months Johnson continued his public silence about the political situation. Obviously, Johnson was dissatisfied with Roosevelt. On the other hand, he was not very impressed by the Republican nominee, Alfred M. Landon. Johnson complained to close associates that he did not consider Landon of presidential timber.(1)

In June, Johnson was stricken by a cerebral vascular stroke which weakened him tremendously, incapacitating him for several months. As a result he could not participate in the campaign. The public as well as Roosevelt and Landon remained unaware of Johnson's condition, however, because of

efforts by his family and staff to keep his illness
secret.(10)   Both Landon and Roosevelt tried personally to
telephone the senator in order to recruit him for their
campaign. Mrs. Johnson merely told them that her husband was
not well and that he was unable to speak to them.  Following
FDR's call, Johnson confessed to his son that he feared that
the president would not believe that he was sick and unable
to campaign for him.  His seclusion and silence was not
ignored by the press.  There were rumors that Johnson would
announce his support of Landon after Labor Day.  Of course,
Johnson denied the allegation.(18)

        Following the election, Johnson ceased all pretense of
friendship and political support of the administration.  When
he was physically able to resume his duties in the Senate, he
returned as an outspoken critic of Roosevelt and his
policies.  No longer describing Roosevelt as a "gallant
gentleman" with insight and courage, Johnson viewed Roosevelt
as a power-hungry politician with "delusions of grandeur."
He told his son:

        [Roosevelt's] mentality is so restless it has to have
        something new daily.  He has delusions of grandeur which
        make him dissatisfied with dealing with domestic problems
        alone, and which will constantly urge a wider field.
        Like Wilson, he'll see himself the arbiter of the world.
        With his power and the vote he has received, the views of
        men like myself will receive scant attention.(1)

        In February, 1936, just a few weeks following his second
inaugural, Roosevelt presented a plan to Congress for the
reorganization of the federal judiciary.  The plan included a
proposal for the enlargement of the Supreme Court from nine
to fifteen members.  From the beginning everyone was aware of
the reason behind Roosevelt's new scheme.  During his past
term the only major barrier to the New Deal had come not from
the Congress, but from the Supreme Court.  Just a few months
earlier the Court had unanimously ruled Roosevelt's National
Industrial Recovery Act unconstitutional.  Many, including
the president, believed that the Court's decision threatened
the remainder of the New Deal's relief and recovery efforts.
Johnson, after reviewing the case, remarked to his son:  "How
strange it is that a modern, progressive, sensible,
presumably intelligent government, rests in its final
analysis for the determination of social questions and the
policies to be pursued for humanity upon the veto power of
nine old men. . . ."(1)

        Nonetheless, despite his disagreement with the Court's
decision, Johnson was shocked by the president's new scheme.
He viewed Roosevelt's "court packing plan," as it was called
by the opposition, as one of the most flagrant attempts by a
president to dominate all three branches of government.
Johnson was determined to fight him with all his strength.
"We're on the road to Fascism," Johnson wrote, and "with his

reaching into the Supreme Court by his thinly disguised message of yesterday, he will make himself an absolute dictator in fact."(1)

Surprisingly, Johnson discovered a large number of his colleagues, many of them Democrats, supporting his view. The Los Angeles *Times*, which traditionally had been one of the senator's most vocal critics, reversed itself by commending him on his announcement to oppose the measure. Within weeks Johnson had collected clippings from over ten different major newspapers around the country expressing support for his position. By the end of April Johnson had submitted to the Senate over 75,000 signatures and was hoping to increase that to well over 100,000.(1)

Unwilling to surrender to the growing opposition against his plan, the president enlisted the support of Robert La Follette, Jr. from Wisconsin, Hugo Black from Alabama (later appointed a Supreme Court justice), and Joseph Robinson from Arkansas, to lead the administration forces in the Senate. Both La Follette and Black also agreed to embark on a speaking tour in support of the measure. Following the announcement of meetings by the proponents to be held in Los Angeles, San Francisco, and other major cities, Johnson revealed to his son that, "if I was at myself I would follow them along, as I followed Wilson in 1919 and 1920. I know there is sufficient sentiment in the country upon this issue to give large meetings. . ."(1) Unfortunately, Johnson did not feel physically strong enough for such an adventure. He admitted privately to his family that he was having difficulty following and developing the logical structure of arguments.(1) Not able to respond in person, Johnson chose to "go on the radio for thirty minutes" in order to answer their claims.(18)

Although originally pessimistic about the chance of winning, Johnson became somewhat more optimistic in May when the administration forces offered to discuss a compromise. Johnson viewed this new move as a sign that the proponents were weakening. They offered to reduce the original proposal of fifteen members to only eleven if the opposition would agree to support them. Characteristically, Johnson refused to compromise and declared that any effort to come to an agreement was "disgraceful and humiliating to both sides." As far as Johnson was concerned, whether the plan proposed six or two new members, it was still a "crime against democracy."(1) Both the Washington *Post* and the Washington *Herald*, following the senator's refusal to consider a compromise, applauded him for remaining firm.

Johnson's tenacity over the Court issue eventually prevailed. The administration forces capitulated on July 22, 1937, by allowing the measure to be referred back to committee. Johnson immediately exclaimed, "Glory be to God!"(321) His declaration was followed by applause from the

Senate chambers. After having received several letters of congratulation, Johnson told his son that he did not think that a two-hour speech could have created as much attention as his short exclamation had achieved.(1)

Roosevelt's failure to reorganize the Court was a major blow to the administration. According to William Leuchtenburg, the issue significantly decreased the unity of the Democratic party, alienated many Progressives, and helped to promote the forming of a bipartisan anti-New Deal coalition in Congress.(187) It also destroyed Johnson's friendship with Roosevelt.

In the years that followed, Johnson opposed and voted against every major piece of legislation supported by the administration. He voted against the executive reorganization bill, the Fair Labor Standards Act, the farm bill of 1937, the lending-spending measure, appropriations for public works, and the housing bill of 1939. He voted against them, not because he was against legislation aimed at helping the poor and unemployed, but because these measures increased executive power. He explained to his son that "while anxious to relieve the destitute," he could not vote for any bill that gave the president too much power over economic policy. He warned that unless something happened to stop Roosevelt, the country was destined to become "totalitarian or Fascist."(1) Pretentiously, Johnson viewed himself as one of the sole remaining bastions safeguarding the nation against a despotic president with personal aspirations for world greatness.

On the international front, the civilized world appeared to be teetering on the edge of disaster. Italy marched into Ethiopia, Germany into the Rhineland, and Japan into Manchuria. War seemed imminent. As these events were occurring, Roosevelt was clamoring for greater discretionary power to deal with these situations. Following the Ethiopian crisis Roosevelt sought a revision of the Neutrality Act of 1935 that would incorporate a new provision empowering the president to impose discretionary embargoes on raw materials. Johnson, an advocate of absolute neutrality, viewed Roosevelt's request as equivalent to granting the president the right to negotiate and to sign an implicit alliance with one of the belligerent nations involved in the conflict. Johnson was convinced that the president's proposal would lead to war rather than prevent it.(1)

Immediately following Roosevelt's "quarantine" speech in Chicago on October 5, 1938, Johnson presented a resolution of inquiry into foreign policy agreements with Britain. He termed the president's speech "irresponsible" and demanded that Roosevelt respond to allegations that he had agreed to back Britain against Japan should a conflict arise.(323) In the months that followed Johnson continued to hammer away at Roosevelt's foreign policy. He was convinced that Roosevelt was leading the nation into an unwanted war. The world situation revitalized Johnson. He told his son in March, 1938, that he felt much stronger and capable of presenting a lengthy address, something he had not been able to do since his stroke two years earlier.(1)

Johnson's attacks against the president reached a climax in February, 1939, when Roosevelt informed the Senate Foreign Relations Committee, chaired by Johnson, about a proposed French purchase of planes from this country. The Washington News quoted Johnson as he asked the president, "Are we on the road to war?" A few days later he lamented to his son that "the lines are divided" and that Roosevelt was "willing to fight to the last American, both Germany and Italy."(1) He told the press that "President Roosevelt is using dictatorial tactics to keep his foreign policy secret and is risking American involvement in war through clandestine international deals."(18) A few weeks later, while speaking against the "cashandcarry" plan, proposed by Senator Key Pittman, Democrat from Nevada, Johnson warned that the selling of war materials to belligerents would make this country "the ally of Japan in the Pacific and Great Britain in the Atlantic."(328) Only weeks later Hitler shocked the world by his attack on Poland. But Johnson was not surprised. He had predicted the event five months earlier.(1) Although Johnson, like most Americans, detested and denounced Hitler's action, he still repeated his pleas for the United States to stay out of the war. In 1940, Johnson sought a fifth term in the Senate and pledged to fight with all his power any plan for the United States to declare war on Germany.

As in 1934, Johnson had little difficulty winning reelection. Shortly after his announcement that he was a candidate, he was endorsed by the California State Federation of Labor. In addition, Johnson was supported by several newspapers, including the Los Angeles Times, which declared that "he has shown himself to be a patriotic American of unquestioned influence." Despite the fact that Johnson did not set foot in his home state, he won the nomination in the Republican, Democratic, and Progressive party primaries overwhelmingly. Following the primary results and in honor of his seventy-fourth birthday, Newsweek proclaimed:  "Last week, as a birthday present to their hero the voters gave Johnson a 4 to 1 margin in the GOP primary over three opponents combined, a clear majority over five rivals in the Democratic race, and the Progressive nomination as well."

With his own reelection in the bag Johnson agreed to support the Republican presidential candidate, although admittedly, he was far from enthusiastic. Johnson told his son that Willkie had eliminated every significant issue with which he might challenge his opponent.(1) Nonetheless, Johnson was willing to support anyone over Roosevelt.

Unable because of his age to participate in a nationwide

stump campaign Johnson agreed to make an address over national radio. The address was presented, October 24, 1940, over the CBS Radio network. Johnson centered his attack on the issue of a third term and argued that Presidents Jefferson, Madison, Monroe, Jackson, and Cleveland had all supported limiting a president to only two terms. As Johnson explained, "Power is a deadly wine. Few human brains can resist it. And certainly there has been no evidence or even desire of resistance in the gentleman who seeks it now."(333)

Johnson was surprised by the public's response to his address. He received thousands of letters agreeing with his position. Two weeks later, Life magazine, October 28, 1940, published an article about Johnson's radio address. The story pictured Johnson in front of the microphone and described his style: "If the radio were a device for bridging time as well as space, many an American might well have imagined as he sat by his loud-speaker on the evening of October 18 that he was listening to the voice of Daniel Webster, Henry Clay, or John C. Calhoun." Despite Johnson's efforts, Roosevelt was elected for a third term.

As the Seventy-seventh Congress convened on January 3, 1941, the war in Europe overshadowed all other important issues. France had fallen to the Germans, while Great Britain desperately fought to prevent what many thought was an inevitable defeat. Roosevelt, fearing the consequences of a British defeat, proposed his lend-lease plan to Congress, declaring that the United States should be the "great arsenal of democracy." Johnson thought the plan to be tantamount to declaring war. He called lend-lease the "wickedest piece of legislation that has ever been presented to the American Congress"(1) and warned that if approved it would inevitably lead to America's involvement. Behind the president's proposal, Johnson saw the devious plotting of Winston Churchill, whom he described as a "cross between a spider and a hog." These two men, Roosevelt and Churchill, Johnson believed were conspiring to force the United States into the war.(1)

Along with Senator Borah, Johnson led the fight against lend-lease. As a means of inciting public opposition to Roosevelt's plan, Johnson presented an address on the National Radio Forum which was broadcast over the NBC radio network. Despite Johnson's efforts, the Senate approved the measure by a vote of 60 to 31. Disillusioned and tired following the outcome of the debate, Johnson wrote bitterly: "Last night we did the dirty deed. We assassinated liberty under the pretext of aiding a belligerent in the war."(1) Although discouraged and pessimistic about the future, Johnson continued throughout the remaining months of 1941 to issue his warning of the impending danger facing the United States.

Finally, on December 7, 1941, Johnson's persistent fight

for strict neutrality was ended abruptly by the Japanese attack on Pearl Harbor. Johnson's fight had been a long and bitter battle. For two decades he had fought unrelentlessly for neutrality. A few days later, on December 11, 1941, Johnson, for the second time in his long career, joined with an almost unanimous Congress in voting for a declaration of war. In the months that followed Johnson faithfully supported the war effort, although he did not play a significant role in it.

Due to poor health, Johnson's participation in the Senate decreased significantly during the war. According to his own accounts, his mind often wandered during committee meetings, he had difficulty organizing his thoughts and remembering important details, and difficulty delivering his speeches. By 1942 Johnson was so physically weak that he could no longer walk the two blocks from his home to his office in the Capitol Building.(1) In 1943 he was hospitalized for a stroke which kept him paralyzed for several weeks. He was not allowed to return home until the middle of September and then, only under the condition that he remain in bed each day until noon and limit his activities in the Senate to afternoon sessions. By 1944, Johnson was no longer an active member of Congress. Nevertheless, he refused to give in to his physical impairment.

During the summer of 1945 he attended the Senate proceedings on the proposal to create the United Nations. Although sick and barely able to hear or speak, Johnson voiced his opposition to the proposed international organization. On July 13, 1945, Johnson was the only dissenting vote in the Foreign Relations Committee against ratification of the United Nations Charter.

Shortly thereafter, Johnson was again forced to return to the Bethesda Naval Hospital for treatment. While confined to his bed, Johnson registered his last vote against American participation in the United Nations. A few days later, August 6, 1945, on the same day that the United States dropped the atomic bomb on Hiroshima, Johnson died of a cerebral thrombosis.(3e)

As a legacy to future generations Johnson left his private papers and the transcripts of many of his public addresses. These documents provide a key to understanding the man, his beliefs, and the times in which he lived. In the final analysis, Johnson's career ended as it had begun, in opposition. Undoubtedly, Johnson will be labelled an isolationist and remembered as a major proponent of neutrality. But as a politician Johnson should also be remembered as he perceived himself, as a champion of the common people battling against the political corruption of big business, as a proponent of progressivism, and as a defender of civil liberties. At the same time, while he was moved by the suffering of the masses, he was not bound by

their transient impressions. As an orator, his speeches
typified progressive rhetoric, and his speaking ability was
largely responsible for his political success.

# 2

# Works about Johnson

## Special Collections

001.  Hiram W. Johnson Papers (C-B 581).    The Bancroft
Library, University of California, Berkeley.

The Bancroft Library obtained the  personal papers of
Johnson in 1955.   This extensive collection includes
private letters to family members (open to the public in
1966) and letters to friends and political associates.
Also included are manuscripts and transcripts of many of
his speeches, press releases, campaign material,
scrapbooks, motion pictures, and a large collection of
newspaper and magazine clippings about Johnson dating from
1885 to 1945.    Drafts of a proposed biography of his
father and notes taken at the 1920 National Republican
Convention written by Hiram, Jr. are available.    The
papers are arranged chronologically and divided by the
types of materials described above.   An excellent index to
the papers aids the researcher.

002.  Burke, Robert E. (ed.).    The Diary Letters of Hiram
Johnson.   New York: Garland Publishing, Inc., 1983, 7 Vols.

A portion of the Hiram Johnson papers, these letters were
written by Johnson on an almost weekly basis to his sons,
Hiram, Jr. and Archibald, detailing political events and
vividly describing those with whom he was working.
National and international topics were discussed as were
family business, illnesses, celebrations, etc.   Burke also
provides an informative summary of Johnson's career and
introductions to the various Congresses in which Johnson
served.   A useful index is provided.

003.  Newspapers.

The following newspapers are especially helpful in
illuminating Johnson's career and often published his
speeches or excerpts of speeches:

<table>
<tr><td>(a) Chicago Tribune</td><td>(g) Sacramento Bee</td></tr>
<tr><td>(b) Fresno Republican</td><td>(h) Sacramento Record-Union</td></tr>
<tr><td>(c) Los Angeles Express</td><td>(i) San Francisco Bulletin</td></tr>
<tr><td>(d) Los Angeles Times</td><td>(j) San Francisco Call</td></tr>
<tr><td>(e) New York Times</td><td>(k) San Francisco Chronicle</td></tr>
<tr><td>(f) Philadelphia North American</td><td>(l) Washington Times</td></tr>
</table>

## General Perspectives

004. Anonymous. "Hiram Johnson, A Champion of Progressivism." United States News, 2 (11 June 1934), 10.

This short biography of Johnson traces his life from his early education to his authorship of the Johnson Act, "retaliating against war debtors in default." Johnson is active in the Senate chamber: "He does not have to read the Congressional Record to find out what has happened. He was there when it occurred. . . ."

005. Boyle, Peter Gerard. "The Study of an Isolationist: Hiram Johnson." Ph.D. Thesis. University of California, Los Angeles, 1970.

Boyle provides an extensive analysis of Johnson's role in the development of American foreign policy between 1917 and 1945. Writing from a pro-Wilson and internationalist view, Boyle claims, "Much of Johnson's thinking and many of his basic attitudes were developed in the days of World War I." Thus, Johnson "stood for the value of an older America which he did not wish to see destroyed by involvement in war and foreign entanglements."

006. Burke, Robert E. "A Friendship in Adversity: Burton K. Wheeler [and] Hiram W. Johnson." Montana, 36 (Winter 1986), 12-25.

In spite of age and party differences Johnson and Wheeler were close friends and political allies. In the 1920s they supported the labor movement and social legislation; they opposed Harding and Coolidge on almost every issue. In the 1930s they voted together for most New Deal legislation and broke with FDR over the Supreme Court reorganization. Both opposed changes in neutrality legislation and, in 1941, they worked together against the lend-lease proposal.

007. Cain, Earl R. "Hiram Johnson: Irreconcilable Isolationist," in David H. Grover (ed.). Landmarks in Western Oratory. Laramie: Univ. of Wyoming Press, 1968, pp. 145-157.

Cain examines the doctrine of isolationism as Johnson presented it in speeches between 1919 and 1945. He sees Johnson's early speeches as being a reflection of popular opinion. When war broke out in Europe in 1939, however, Johnson found himself more and more in the minority, but he refused to change his position, even opposing ratification of the UN Charter.

008. DeWitt, Howard A.  "Hiram W. Johnson and American Foreign Policy, 1917-1941." Ph.D. Thesis. University of Arizona, 1972.

According to DeWitt, Johnson's only significant contribution to American foreign policy was the Johnson Act of 1934. He was, however, "a publicist and polemicist for isolation." Based primarily on Johnson's personal correspondence, DeWitt offers both "positive and negative aspects" of the senator's isolationist policies.

009. Dillon, Richard. Humbugs and Heroes: A Gallery of California Pioneers. Garden City, NY: Doubleday & Co., 1970, pp. 177-81, 347, 348.

After reciting some of Johnson's accomplishments, Dillon suggests that by 1920 Johnson's reforming zeal had ended and that throughout his senate career he took a conservative political stance. Johnson's stand against the League of Nations and in opposition to FDR's foreign policy are cited examples of the now conservative Johnson.

010. Fitzpatrick, John J.  "Senator Hiram W. Johnson: A Life History, 1866-1945." Ph.D. Thesis. University of California, Berkeley, 1975.

Fitzpatrick's work is a psycho-biography of Johnson.  The author discusses in detail Johnson's relationship with his father and what influence it had on Johnson's political views.  In addition, the thesis offers a chronological description of Johnson's career. Included are extensive excerpts from his private letters, papers, and speeches.

011. Ickes, Harold L. The Autobiography of a Curmudgeon. New York: Reynal and Hitchcock, 1943, pp. 163, 181-183, 222-238, 246-253, 264-268, 270-271.

Written by a political and personal friend of Johnson, Ickes' autobiography provides an insider's view of the political scene from 1912 to the early 1940s. Especially noteworthy are Ickes' accounts of the 1920 Republican presidential nominating convention and the 1924 Illinois Republican primary where he served as Johnson's campaign manager. Johnson supported Ickes' efforts to be secretary of the interior in Franklin Roosevelt's cabinet.

012. Johnson, Robert S.  "Senator Hiram Johnson and American Foreign Affairs." M.A. Thesis. University of California, Berkeley, 1945.

Johnson expressed the "attitudes of the masses: their fears of the foreigner, their suspicions of diplomats, their dread of war, their most compelling of all drives, self-interest, their strongest of all sentiments, love of home and country." He formed his judgments quickly and reduced complicated problems to moral terms.

013.  Lower, Richard C.  "Hiram Johnson and the Progressive Denouement, 1910-1920." Ph.D. Thesis.  University of California, Berkeley, 1969.

Concentrating on the years 1910-1920, Lower finds Johnson's career marked by failure--failure to overthrow the established party system and failure to put progressive principles into effect on the national level. The battle against the League of Nations was a "sacrifice of Progressive resources" and led to the denouement of the movement.

014. Lowry, Edward G.  "Hiram W. Johnson." Colliers, 65 (21 February 1920), 16.

Lowry visited Sacramento to talk to friends of Johnson in order to provide an intimate portrait of the presidential candidate.  Finding amusing anecdotes about Johnson proved difficult, but Lowry discovered the story of Johnson's boyhood recitation of "Sheridan's Last Ride" to General Grant.  Johnson's early career and the graft trials are narrated. Johnson is a motion picture fan and "the best domino player in the world." Lowry concludes: "He is an honest, outspoken man with the bark on. You won't have to puzzle out the meaning of what he says."

015.  Mowry, George E.    The California Progressives. Berkeley: University of California Press, 1951.

Mowry attempts to discover who the Progressives were, what prompted them to act, and what they were trying to do by focusing on the California progressive movement from 1900 to 1916.  Especially noteworthy are Mowry's descriptions of Johnson's gubernatorial campaign of 1910, Johnson's role in the emergence and decline of the National Progressive Party, and the split between the Johnson faction and the regular Republican party which led to the defeat of Charles Evans Hughes in the presidential election of 1916.  Mowry finds that ". . . the national Progressive leaders were extraordinarily individualistic and his character was marked by a pronounced ambitious and competitive strain.  He was usually highly intolerant of opposition either from within or without his own ranks. . . .  Certainly many of those characteristics were found in Hiram Johnson."

016. Mowry, George E.  "Hiram Johnson." in Edward T. James, et al., (eds.).  Dictionary of American Biography.  Supplement

Three.   New York:  Charles  Scribner's  Sons,  1973,  pp.  393-398.

Mowry  provides  an  excellent  summary  of  Johnson's  career,
his  terms  as  governor,  his  interests  in  domestic  concerns
and  foreign  affairs  while  in  the  Senate,  and  his  support
for  and  finally  disillusionment  with  FDR.   Mowry  suggests
that  Johnson  viewed  politics  in  very  personal  terms  and
that  by  the  close  of  his  career  "a  lonely  negativism  had
become  almost  ingrained."   Nevertheless,  California
respected  his  incorruptible  independence.

017.   Tucker,  Ray  and  Frederick  R.  Barkley.   Sons  of  the  Wild
Jackass.   Boston:   LC  Page,  1932.   Reprinted  Seattle:
University  of  Washington  Press,  1970,  pp.  xxi,  xxii,  7,  8,
11,  13,  14,  31,  38,  83,  96-122,  336,  337.

Johnson  is  one  of  fifteen  "mules"  whose  political  career
is  related.   Highly  favorable  and  with  an  eye  toward
detail,  they  describe  Johnson  as  "a  fighter,  a  reformer,  a
strong  character,  a  brilliant  executive. . . ."   The  way
the  authors  picture  Johnson's  rejection  of  Harding's  offer
of  the  vice  presidency  in  1920  is  must  reading.   Personal
notes,  from  Johnson's  favorite  breed  of  dog  (Pekingese)  to
the  pictures  on  his  Senate  office  wall,  abound.

018.   Weatherson,  Michael  A.   "Political  Revivalist:  The
Public  Speaking  of  Hiram  W.  Johnson,  1866-1945."   Ph.D.
Thesis.   Indiana  University,  1985.

This  work  is  a  critical  analysis  of  Johnson's  public
speaking  within  the  historical  context  of  the  period.   The
chapters  are  divided  chronologically  into  the  major  issues
of  Johnson's  career.   Included  are  excerpts  from  newspaper
coverage  of  Johnson's  campaigns  and  public  speeches,  his
personal  letters,  and  the  Congressional  Record.

## The Roots of Insurgency: Johnson's Early Career

019.   Bean,  Walton  E.   Boss  Ruef's  San  Francisco:   The  Story
of  the  Union  Labor  Party,  Big  Business,  and  the  Graft
Prosecution.   Berkeley:  University  of  California  Press,  1967,
pp.  65,  162-163,  166,  180-184,  223,  285-286,  305-306,  314.

Bean  discusses  Johnson's  role  in  the  graft  prosecution
trial  of  Abe  Ruef  of  San  Francisco.   Johnson  aided  Francis
Heney  before  the  grand  jury  and  took  over  the  prosecution
duties  of  Ruef's  trial  when  Heney  was  shot.   Found  guilty
of  bribery,  Ruef  was  sentenced  to  fourteen  years  in  San
Quentin.

020.   Irvine,  Leigh  H.   A  History  of  the  New  California.   New
York:  The  Lewis  Publishing  Company,  1905,  pp.  472-475.

Irvine  provides  a  short  biographical  sketch  of  Johnson's father, Grove Lawrence Johnson. The praise is often overwhelming: "It is our duty to mark our appreciation of such a man, a man true in every relation of life, faithful to every trust, a statesman diligent in the service of his country and seeking only the public good." Nevertheless, the important political and social events in Grove Johnson's life are chronicled.

021. McKee, Irving. "The Background and Early Career of Hiram Warren Johnson, 1866-1910." Pacific Historical Review, 19 (January 1950), 17-30.

McKee's portrait takes Johnson from birth to his decision to campaign for governor in 1910. Grove Johnson's political career is detailed as is Hiram's early legal career. Although Hiram and his brother Albert first supported Grove, they eventually opposed him as a tool of the railroad interests. Hiram became a leader of the progressive Lincoln-Roosevelt Republican League and reluctantly agreed to be their candidate for governor.

022. Storke, Thomas M. California Editor. Los Angeles: Westernlore Press, 1958, pp. 6, 153, 157, 165, 177-78, 180-97, 201, 246, 343-349, 397, 399, 406, 432, 439.

Storke, editor of the Santa Barbara News-Press, was a long-time friend and admirer of Johnson. Grove Johnson, Hiram's father, was Storke's house guest at the time Hiram agreed to prosecute Abe Ruef whom Grove threatened to defend. Storke reviews Johnson's career as governor and relates Johnson's activities during the banking crisis of 1933 as one who was present during some of the negotiations attempting to keep the Bank of America open.

## Kick the Southern Pacific Out of Politics: Johnson for Governor

023. Anonymous. "California Clings to Her Parties." Literary Digest, 51 (13 November 1915), 1069.

California's rejection of Johnson's plan to make all state office elections nonpartisan is discussed. Johnson's reaction is quoted as are opposition views. The election loss was seen as the end of progressive experiments in California.

024. Anonymous. "Hiram Johnson, Political Revivalist." American Review of Reviews, 46 (September 1912), 306-309.

The author praises Johnson for his role in the San Francisco graft prosecutions and for the progressive legislation passed in California. A number of quotations describing Johnson's effective speaking style are offered.

025. Anonymous.   "How Hiram Johnson Broke the Power of the Southern Pacific."  Current Opinion, 62 (April 1917), 245-246.

The author relates Burton J. Hendrick's account of Johnson's first gubernatorial campaign.  Johnson travelled across the state in an automobile with a cowbell attached to attract voters to his meetings.  Johnson's main campaign promise was to drive the Southern Pacific Railroad out of California political life.

026. Bailey, Thomas A.   "California, Japan, and the Alien Land Legislation of 1913."  Pacific Historical Review, 1 (March 1932), 36-59.

Early in 1913 Johnson changed his attitude from opposition to land legislation to support and played a leading role in pushing the Webb bill through the California legislature.  This act provided that aliens could own land only as specified in existing treaties.  Since the treaty with Japan did not provide for ownership of agricultural land, Japanese aliens were barred from owning such land in California.  Wilson sent Secretary of State William Jennings Bryan to California to meet with the state legislature, but he was unsuccessful in his attempt to delay action or to amend the bill to mollify the Japanese.

027. Beatty, Bessie.  What Will Women do to Repay Hiram Johnson?"  No publisher, 1914 [?].

In this 1914 campaign document, Beatty argues that women owe the eight-hour day and the right to vote to Johnson. She finds in California "the most complete revolution of the social and economic status of women ever produced in an American commonwealth."  A vote for Johnson is "a vote for women's humanitarian policy in government."

028. Caughey, John W. California: History of a Remarkable State.  4th Edition.  Edgewood Cliffs, N.J.: Prentice-Hall, 1982, pp. 284, 288-291.

Led by Johnson, the Lincoln-Roosevelt League captured the popular imagination and with Johnson's election as governor in 1910 was able to pass a number of political and social reforms.  By 1914, however, they had been so successful that they ran out of new ideas and deep rifts developed within the group.  Johnson was the only one of the leaders to move on in public office.

029. Creel, George.   "What About Hiram Johnson of California?"  Everybody's, 31 (1914), 448-460.

While admiring much of the progressive legislation passed in California between 1910 and 1914, Creel argues that Johnson had little responsibility for it. John R. Haynes deserves credit as the "Father of the Initiative, Referendum, and Recall." Johnson was a late-comer to the progressive movement. In a harsh indictment of Johnson, Creel declares: "That he has so utterly failed to give proper public credit, extend appreciation, or withhold self-laudation, is an even harsher indictment against Hiram Johnson than his failure to cast his fortunes with the forward movement in the days when it seemed a forlorn hope."

030. Daniels, Roger. The Politics of Prejudice. Berkeley: University of California Press, 1962, pp. 47, 49-69, 79, 82, 95, 96, 98, 100, 112-117.

Johnson's failure to court the anti-Japanese vote may have cost him votes in the gubernatorial election of 1910 and he pointedly ignored the Japanese question in his inaugural address. Johnson, however, regarded the passage of the 1913 anti-Japanese land bill as a political triumph, feeling it would never again be a political question in California. Appendix B contains a letter from Johnson to Theodore Roosevelt explaining the struggle between himself and Wilson and Bryan.

031. Hendrick, Burton J. "Johnson of California." The World's Work, 33 (January 1917), 289-294.

Hendrick offers an excellent synopsis of the progressive legislation Johnson supported as governor and details the campaign that elected him to office. According to Hendrick, "Johnson went out, like a Salvation Army revivalist, in the pursuit of political souls." Hendrick blames Hughes' election defeat on his ignoring of the Johnson element in the Republican party.

032. Hichborn, Franklin, "The Party, the Machine, and the Vote." California Historical Society Quarterly, 39 (1960), 19-34.

Hichborn argues that Johnson was able to be elected governor because of the recently passed direct primary bill. Once elected, Johnson tried to make state and county elections nonpartisan. California voters turned down a nonpartisan direct primary for state offices but eventually allowed candidates to have their names appear on the primary ballots of parties other than their own.

033. Hichborn, Franklin. Story of the California Legislature of 1911. San Francisco: James H. Barry Company, 1911, pp. 11-12, 21, 23, 40-49, 325-326, 343-344, appendix i-xviii.

The November 1910 elections in California not only brought Johnson to the governor's office, but swept out a number of "machine" members of the senate and assembly. Men in sympathy with progressive ideals became chairs of the various committees which at Johnson's urging reported bills calling for the initiative, referendum, recall, direct vote for senators, and effective railroad legislation. The appendix contains Johnson's inaugural address and his message on the state prison employment bill.

034. Hichborn, Franklin. Story of the Sessions of the California Legislature of 1913. San Francisco: James H. Barry Company, 1913, pp. 19, 23, 70, 77-80, 85-86, 137-138, 246-248, 257-258, appendix ii-ix.

Johnson's response to many of the acts of the legislature is given, especially with regard to the anti-Japanese alien land legislation. The appendix contains Johnson's reply to Secretary of State Bryan in which he indicates that he will sign the bill as passed by the legislature.

035. Hudson, James J. "California National Guard and the Mexican Border." California Historical Society Quarterly, 34 (June 1955), 157-171.

Johnson received a number of requests in the spring of 1914 to send the California National Guard to the Mexican Border to protect Americans in the Imperial Valley from Mexican raiders. Troops were eventually mustered and equipped under the supervision of the U.S. Army.

036. Hundley, Norris C., Jr. "Katherine Philips Edson and the Fight for the California Minimum Wage, 1912-1923." Pacific Historical Review, 29 (August 1960), 271-285.

Edson headed the list of Governor Johnson's appointees to the first California Labor Bureau. Johnson did not approve of women in government, but he admired Edson for her work in campaigning for a minimum wage for women and minors.

037. Kent, William. "Johnson of California." The Outlook, 100 (10 February 1912), 313-319.

Elected governor in 1910 on the platform of kicking the Southern Pacific Railroad out of state politics, Johnson forced those officials who owed their jobs to the railroad to resign or convinced the legislature to abolish their positions. Johnson's inaugural address provided a clearcut outline of what he hoped to accomplish (e.g., direct election of senators, shortening the ballot, prison reform, etc.) Kent describes the work of the legislature, as well as Johnson's personal characteristics which helped him lead it to pass a host of progressive ideas.

038. Knoche, Viola. "The Gubernatorial Nomination of Hiram W. Johnson, 1910." M.A. Thesis. Stanford University, August

1967.

Knoche's work concentrates on Johnson's 1910 gubernatorial campaign, providing a comparison of Johnson's campaign strategy and speaking style with that of his opponents such as Theodore Bell, the Democratic candidate. Knoche relies heavily on media coverage of the election and includes significant excerpts from local and regional newspapers.

039. La Pore, Herbert P. "Prelude to Prejudice: Hiram Johnson, Woodrow Wilson, and the California Alien Land Law Controversy of 1913." Southern California Quarterly, 61 (Spring 1979), 99-110.

According to La Pore, "Progressives in California believed that economic self-preservation was closely united with racial preservation." Economic inroads by the Japanese would lead to racial inroads. Johnson was the stimulus that influenced the California legislature to pass anti-Japanese land ownership legislation. Standing up to President Wilson offered a way for him to show leadership and power while supporting a measure his constituents desired.

040. Layne, J. Gregg. "The Lincoln-Roosevelt League: Its Origin and Accomplishments." Southern California Quarterly, 25 (September 1943), 79-101.

Layne considers Johnson, "the greatest platform orator that the country had ever produced." After a description of Johnson's campaign for governor, Layne lists 25 "notable accomplishments" of his legislative program.

041. Melendy, Howard B., and Benjamin F. Gilbert. The Governors of California. Georgetown, CA: The Talisman Press, 1965, pp. 269, 286, 300, 306-321, 324, 350, 352-353, 427, 428.

Johnson's administration as governor (1911-1917) is said to have "changed the character and structure of California life and politics." Melendy reviews the long list of progressive legislation that Johnson encouraged and eventually signed into law. Under Johnson's administration, state government was reorganized and became better able to handle contemporary problems. Johnson "must rank as one of California's greatest governors."

042. Olin, Spencer C., Jr. California's Prodigal Sons: Hiram Johnson and the Progressives, 1911-1917. Berkeley: University of California Press, 1968.

An excellent account of the growth and success of the Lincoln-Roosevelt League, the political organization most responsible for Johnson's victory in 1910.  Johnson's gubernatorial campaign is described in detail and Olin provides insight into the reasons for the progressive movement's success.  The reader is also provided with a vivid description of the personalities of each of the major participants in the movement.  In addition, Olin describes the failure of the Progressives to achieve national success in 1912 and offers reasons for the decline of the movement.

043.  Olin, Spencer C., Jr.  "Hiram Johnson, the California Progressives, and the Hughes Campaign of 1916."  Pacific Historical Review, 31 (November 1962), 403-412.

By placing himself in the hands of regular Republicans while he was in California from August 17 through August 22, presidential candidate Charles Evans Hughes alienated Johnson's supporters and cost himself the 1916 election.

044.  Olin, Spencer C., Jr.  "Hiram Johnson, the Lincoln-Roosevelt League, and the Election of 1910."  California Historical Society Quarterly, 45 (September 1966), 225-240.

Johnson's flair for generating public enthusiasm made him the ideal candidate of the Lincoln-Roosevelt reform movement for Governor in 1910.  After a series of campaign blunders by the league organization, Johnson set up his own organization and refused to travel with the League's other candidates.  Olin characterizes the campaign as a conflict between one group of capitalists (the large farmers and ranchers) and another group of capitalists (the railroad interests).

045.  Progressive Party of California.  California Progressive Campaign Book for 1914.  San Francisco, 1914.

"Published as a campaign book for the use of editors, speakers, and others supporting the Progressive party of California in 1914," this volume summarizes what the party felt were its major accomplishments, including the modernization of mental hospitals, a new railroad commission, a shortened work day for women, child labor laws, an alien land act, etc.  Included are copies of Johnson's inaugural address as governor on January 3, 1911 and Johnson's denial of Secretary of State William J. Bryan's request that he veto the alien land bill.

046.  Rogin, Michael Paul and John L. Shover.  Political Change in California.  Westport, Conn: Greenwood Pub. Co., 1970, pp. xvii, 37-39, 43-49, 51-53, 55, 63-72, 75-76, 78-80, 82-83, 85, 114, 125, 128, 158.

Johnson's campaign in 1910 appealed most strongly to rural, native-stock Protestant counties and least strongly to Catholics, immigrants, and Bay area residents.  Johnson did well in Southern California, not because he was a Progressive, but because he was a Republican. By 1916 the Bay area was Johnson's major source of supporters. Progressive voters voted for Wilson rather than Hughes while supporting Johnson for the Senate.

047. Rowell, Chester H. "More about Hiram Johnson." Everybody's, 31 (November 1914), 636-639.

Rowell responded to Creel's attack on Johnson (29). Johnson never claimed "sole credit" for the progressive accomplishments of his administration. Nor did he labor in "obscurity" before his election to the governorship. He took an active leadership role in the campaigns of Taylor, Langdon, Leland, and Heney. Creel's facts are wrong and he was influenced "by a bias which he brought with him to California."

048. Sinclair, Andrew. Prohibition: The Era of Excess. Boston: Little Brown & Co., 1962, p. 96

The Anti-Saloon League and the vote of dry Los Angeles supported Johnson in the election of 1910, but Progressives split along the urban-rural lines in 1911 over a county option measure.

049. Smith, Geddes. "California Progressivism." The Independent, 83 (August 1915), 296-297.

Smith interviewed Johnson about the prospects of progressivism in California and in the nation. Johnson was confident: "Progressivism will go on. . . . If the Progressive party should disintegrate tomorrow I am confident that there will be enough progressives in the other parties to carry on the work. . . ."

050. Strother, E. French. "Hiram W. Johnson, the Man." California Weekly, (25 February 1910), 219-220.

This character sketch of Johnson as candidate for governor provides some interesting anecdotes of his college days at Berkeley and his early political career. Johnson entered the race for governor reluctantly. Johnson's creed is the "destruction of the power of the Southern Pacific's Political Bureau and the emancipation of the state from corporate control."

051. Williams, Edgar. "The Man Who Swept California." The Outlook, 114 (22 November 1916), 639-644.

This "personal sketch of Hiram W. Johnson" is just that--a personal look at the political man. Johnson's house is described; his pet name for his wife ("Boss") is revealed; his personal appearance is pictured in great detail; he enjoys baseball games; he has a sense of humor. Johnson's platform manner is described: "He uses few gestures. His most characteristic one is a downward drive with his right arm and closed hand." Williams summarizes Johnson's gubernatorial campaign and provides a list of legislation signed during Governor Johnson's administration.

## A Crusader for a New Cause: Johnson for Vice President

052. Anonymous. "In the Public Eye: A Fighting Progressive." The Outlook, 102 (28 September 1912), 219-220.

After reviewing Johnson's accomplishments as governor of California, the author considers his prospects for the presidency. Much credit for his political success is given to Johnson's speechmaking ability.

053. Anonymous. "Johnson of California: A Progressive in a Hurry." Current Literature, 53 (1 August 1912), 156-159.

The author presents a vivid description of Johnson's speaking style: "His voice sounds just as an east wind feels. It grates and snarls and pierces, and puts you all on edge. The whole man goes with the voice. Every posture and gesture is one of intensity." Johnson gives immediate opinions and calls for immediate action. It is difficult to get Johnson to change his mind on any issue.

054. Bryan, William Jennings. A Tale of Two Conventions. New York: Funk and Wagnalls Co., 1912. Reprinted, New York: Arno Press, 1974, pp. ix, x, 11, 72-74, 248, 303.

The three-time Democratic nominee for president viewed the Republican, Democratic, and Progressive national conventions in 1912 and published daily newspaper accounts of his observations. These accounts were put into book form along with important speeches, party platforms, and contemporary cartoons. Johnson's speech of June 21 was "the gem of the convention so far. . . . He made a plea for the progressive cause that surpassed in effectiveness anything heretofore presented to the delegates."

055. Fausold, Martin L. Gifford Pinchot: Bull Moose Progressive. Syracuse, NY: Syracuse University Press, 1961, pp. 85, 91, 101, 137, 189, 190, 204, 225, 235, 244.

Pinchot delivered one of the nominating speeches for Johnson at the Progressive nominating convention of 1912. Together they worked for Theodore Roosevelt in 1912 and were disappointed when Roosevelt refused to run in 1916.

056. Gable, John Allen. The Bull Moose Years: Theodore Roosevelt and the Progressive Party. Port Washington, NY: Kennikat Press, 1978, pp. 4, 7, 12, 16, 17, 28, 29, 32, 38, 49, 52, 67, 76, 88, 103, 105, 108-109, 111, 123, 135, 136,

144, 170, 179-180, 193, 196, 201, 205, 217, 222-224, 229, 241-242, 246, 249-252.

Hiram Johnson plays a major role in this "case study of a third party." Included in the work are descriptions of behind-the-scene meetings at which Johnson was present. Gable pictures Johnson at the 1912 Republican convention and provides a reporter's description of Johnson's speech. In later years Roosevelt described Johnson as "stubborn and dour, a man driven, fired by righteousness and ambition." Johnson's 1914 description of Amos Pinchot as having become a "terrible and bloodthirsty parlor Anarchist," helps to provide some insight into the division which developed within the party following the 1912 election. Gable also reports that TR suggested Johnson as a presidential candidate in 1916 following his own decision not to run.

057. Garraty, John A., ed. "T.R. on the Telephone." American Heritage, 9 (December 1957), 99-108.

Retired banker, George W. Perkins, installed a private telephone line between his room in the Blackstone Hotel in Chicago and Theodore Roosevelt's Oyster Bay home during the Republican and Progressive parties' conventions in 1916. Johnson's role in the conventions is described by Roosevelt in these transcripts of telephone conversations with a number of Republican and Progressive leaders.

058. Hart, W. O. The Democratic Conventions of 1908, 1912, 1916, and Republican Conventions of 1912, 1916. New Orleans: Private Printing, 1916, pp. 127, 131.

Hart reprints his article from the New Orleans Picayune of August 19, 1912, in which he reports on the Progressive convention of 1912. He suggests that the applause which followed Johnson's acceptance speech "was the most sincere of the entire convention."

059. Lincoln, A. "Theodore Roosevelt, Hiram Johnson, and the Vice-Presidential Nomination of 1912." Pacific Historical Review, 28 (August 1959), 267-283.

Johnson received the Progressive party's nomination for vice president as a result of a five month campaign by his supporters in California, first within the Republican party, and later as Progressives. Johnson's admirers used newspaper editorials, personal appeals, and a stanza from Kipling: "for there is neither East or West, border nor breed nor birth, when two strong men stand face to face, though they come from the ends of the earth," to get their favorite nominated.

060. McGeary, M. Nelson. Gifford Pinchot: Forester-Politician. Princeton, NJ: Princeton Univ. Press, 1960, pp.

225, 227, 231, 251, 253-55, 313, 390.

Pinchot joined Johnson in denouncing the Republican
National Committee in 1912 and in forming the Progressive
party.  Johnson supported Pinchot's unsuccessful campaign
for the senate seat from Pennsylvania in 1914.  In 1924,
Pinchot was rumored for second place on a Republican
ticket headed by Johnson.

061.  Mowry, George E.  Theodore Roosevelt and the
Progressive Movement.  Madison: University of Wisconsin
Press, 1946, pp. 129, 273, 349, 351-353, 363-366, 380.

Roosevelt's refusal of the Progressive party's
presidential nomination in 1916 alienated him from
Johnson.  Mowry describes Johnson's quests for the
Republican and Progressive senatorial nominations in 1916
and his ultimate success at the polls which occurred at
the same time as Charles Evans Hughes was losing the state
and, with it, the presidential election to Wilson.

062.  Pinchot, Amos R.  History of the Progressive Party,
1912-1916.  Westport, Conn: Greenwood Press, 1958, pp. 29,
30, 35, 43, 45, 49, 51, 57, 83, 134-138, 141, 145, 151, 154,
161, 164, 179, 182, 187, 221, 222, 258.

This book includes an introductory biography of Amos
Pinchot (80 pp.) by Helene Hooker providing some insight
into Pinchot's role in the progressive movement and his
relationship to other leaders.  Pinchot gives an indepth
view of the rise and decline of the movement.  Johnson's
role in persuading Roosevelt to run for the presidential
nomination in 1912 and his consequent desertion of
La Follette are discussed.  Pinchot provides an inside
report on what happened in private meetings.  He describes
Johnson's role in the birth of the National Progressive
Party, the 1912 presidential campaign, Johnson's
activities in 1916 during the collapse of the party, and
the campaign for Hughes.

063.  Thelen, David P.  Robert M. La Follette and the
Insurgent Spirit.  Boston: Little, Brown and Company, 1976,
pp. 78, 82, 88, 93-96, 138, 139, 143, 149, 152, 188, 192.

Although Johnson considered La Follette a "pioneer" in the
progressive movement, he much preferred Theodore Roosevelt
to La Follette in the 1912 election causing bitter
feelings between himself and La Follette.  Once elected to
the Senate, Johnson and La Follette worked together to
increase war profits' taxes (1917) and to secure the
withdrawal of American troops from Russia (1919).
La Follette credited Johnson as being one of the major
factors in killing the League of Nations because his
denunciations had stirred up public opinion against the
treaty.

**Back in the Republican Party: Johnson for Senator**

064.   Anonymous.   "The Johnson Victory."   Literary Digest,   53
(23 September 1916), 731-732.

A number of newspaper editorials are quoted to show the
bitterness of the Republican primary election for the
Senate won by Johnson.   The possible effects of Johnson's
candidacy on the presidential campaign of Charles Evans
Hughes are noted.

065.   Anonymous.   "Political Miracles in California."   The
Outlook,   114 (25 October 1916), 412-414.

Johnson's campaign for the Republican nomination for the
U.S.  Senate is reviewed.   Even though voters who were
registered as Progressive could not vote in the Republican
primary, enough regular Republicans voted for Johnson to
give him the victory over Willis H. Booth.   Hughes' vote
in California is in doubt, but Johnson is predicted to win
by at least 100,000 votes.

066.   Cleland, Robert G. From Wilderness to Empire: A History
of California.   Edited by Glenn S. Dumke.   New York: Alfred
Knopf, 1959, pp. 243-247, 250-256, 259, 271, 339, 366, 421.

Cleland recounts Johnson's gubernatorial campaign of 1910
and finds him "an almost ideal candidate for that time and
occasion."   Johnson's Senate career however "was marked by
only two or three significant contributions to the public
good; and that in national politics, the only outstanding
governor California has ever had played the role of
obstructionist and became each year more peevish,
stubborn, and vindictive."   Cleland believes that Johnson
gave only lip service to the candidacy of Hughes in 1916
and thus indirectly encouraged his supporters to vote for
Wilson.   A reconstruction of the Hughes-Johnson "incident"
is provided by Edward Dickson, publisher of the Los
Angeles Evening Express, an eyewitness of the event.

067.   Davenport, Frederick M.   "The Case of Hiram Johnson:
Not Guilty."   North American Review, 205 (1917), 203-220.

Republican conservatives lost the presidential election of
1916 for Hughes.   They controlled Hughes' tour of
California and kept him away from most of the Progressive
leaders.   This may have indicated to voters that Hughes
supported the conservative elements of the party and
favored Johnson's opponent in the Republican primary
election.   Johnson received only 100,000 votes more than
Hughes, probably explained by the "irreducible minimum of
Johnson Democrats, laborites, anti-Hughes women, and
unreconstructed Progressives who were for Johnson, but not
for Hughes."   Davenport provides an interesting response
to Holman.(69)

068.  Davenport, Frederick M.    "The Last Stand of Political
Bourbonism."  The Outlook,  114 (22 November 1916), 644-646.

Hughes lost the presidential election because of the way
reactionary Republican party leaders treated Johnson
during Hughes' campaign visit to California.   Conservative
party leaders (the Bourbons) cost Hughes votes in a number
of other states as well.   Unless progressive Republicans
gain control of the party, Republicans will not win in
1920 because the nation is fast becoming liberal.

069.  Holman, Alfred.    "The Case of Hiram Johnson: Guilty."
North American Review,  205 (1917). 186-202.

Holman sums up his position in these words:   "It was the
deliberate treachery of Governor Johnson and Mr. Rowell
which lost Mr. Hughes the electoral vote of California [in
1916]."  Election returns showed that in those areas in
which the progressive Johnson ran best, Hughes ran the
weakest.   Progressives had taken over the Republican party
through treachery and Johnson, although he said he would
vote for Hughes, refused to campaign for him until it was
too late.   Holman was answered by Davenport.(67)

070. Mayer, George H.   The Republican Party, 1854-1966.   New
York: Oxford University Press, 1967, pp. 292, 316, 330-331,
335, 344-345, 347, 354, 357, 362-363, 366, 371, 376, 387-388,
396, 404, 418-421, 432, 450-451, 461.

Never considered a party regular, Johnson has a
significant impact on the Republican party.   Meyer
discusses Johnson's friction with Charles E. Hughes, his
position on the League of Nations, his attempts at gaining
the Republican presidential nomination, and his
disagreement with Hoover over measures to fight the
depression.   Mayer describes Johnson's position in the
1920s as "obstructionist" and cynical.

## Johnson as an Irreconcilable: Against Wilson and the League

071.  Adler, Selig.   The Isolationist Impulse: Its Twentieth
Century Reaction.  London: Abelard-Schuman Ltd., 1957,  pp.
65, 104, 106, 152, 154, 173-174, 264, 290-291, 354.

Although he admits Johnson was consistent throughout his
political career, Adler believes that Johnson used his
isolationist position to seek the presidency.   According
to Adler, during the League of Nations conflict, Johnson's
"pretentious nationalism" was a "convenient screen" for
his presidential ambitions.   Adler believes that Johnson
hoped that by mixing isolationism with progressive
domestic programs he would appeal to both wings of the
Republican party and capture the Republican presidential
nomination in 1924.

072. Adler, Selig. The Uncertain Giant, 1921-1941: American Foreign Policy Between the Wars. New York: The MacMillan Co., 1965, pp. 11, 65-66, 172, 181-182, 204.

Johnson's speaking tour against the League of Nations was financed by two Pittsburgh multi-millionaires, Henry Clay Frick, and Andrew Mellon. Johnson's campaigning made him a leading contender for the Republican presidential nomination in 1920.

073. Anonymous. "Borah and Johnson, Disturbers of the Senatorial Peace." Literary Digest, 62 (23 August 1919), 52-54.

The author compares Johnson with William Borah of Idaho in terms of philosophy, speaking ability, and political effectiveness. He doubts that either can win the Republican presidential nomination because of their stand against the League of Nations treaty. He mistakenly believes that the treaty will pass with reservations.

074. Anonymous. "Johnson--The only Senator of Whom Wilson Is Afraid." Current Opinion, 67 (October 1919), 224-225.

The author lists important campaign promises made and kept by Johnson. They include state control of banks, insurance for employees, and a corporation tax. Also related is an andecdote about Johnson's relationship with his Chinese cook, which could have cost Johnson labor votes because of strong feelings against the Chinese. Johnson's position on the League of Nations is described.

075. Bailey, Thomas A. Woodrow Wilson and the Great Betrayal. Chicago: Quarangle Books, 1963, pp. 22, 34, 35, 48, 49, 61, 63, 72, 86, 95, 96, 101, 112, 128-129, 133, 158, 162, 208, 220, 228, 282-283, 298-300, 306, 325, 327-329, 377, 380, 402, 405, 414.

Bailey believes that the U.S. should have joined the League so he does not paint a favorable picture of Johnson whom he labels the "noise" of the irreconcilables. Admitting that Johnson held a consistent position throughout his career, Bailey argues that Johnson's opposition was politically motivated. He wanted to be president.

076. Berdahl, Clarence A. The Policy of the United States with Respect to the League of Nations. Geneva: Graduate Institute of International Studies, 1932, pp. 51, 55-56, 63, 68, 76, 94, 118.

Based on a series of lectures at the Graduate Institute of International Studies at Geneva, Berdahl tries to explain why "the nation whose representative was the strongest advocate for a League of Nations, having security for peace as its main object, refuses altogether to join that League." Johnson's role in the Senate is discussed. Johnson wanted the treaty issue made an issue in the presidential campaign of 1920. In 1932 he was still speaking against the League and any form of cooperation with it.

077. Cranston, Alan. The Killing of the Peace. New York: Viking Press, 1945, pp. 5-6.

Cranston has no sympathy for Johnson's position against the League; but, nevertheless, describes his speaking as "an awesome impression of power." Johnson's western tour drew great crowds and his proposed amendment to the treaty to give the United States the same number of votes as the British Empire was barely defeated 38 to 40.

078. DeWitt, Howard A. "Hiram Johnson and World War I: A Progressive in Transition." Southern California Quarterly, 56 (Fall 1974), 295-305.

DeWitt claims that Johnson's isolationism was "the direct result of his reaction to Wilsonian diplomacy." With little knowledge of foreign affairs, Johnson "never bothered to expand his reading habits to include history and political science." Johnson's attitudes toward foreign policy was shaped by his fear of excessive business influence on American foreign policy and by what he considered to be Wilson's abuses of presidential power.

079. DeWitt, Howard A. "Hiram W. Johnson and Economic Opposition to Wilsonian Diplomacy: A Note." The Pacific Historian, 19 (Spring 1975), 15-23.

DeWitt argues that economic fears were at the center of Johnson's opposition to Wilsonian diplomacy. The alleged influences of bankers and businessmen on American foreign policy coupled with Wilson's knowledge of secret agreements between the Allied powers and Japan led Johnson to oppose the Versailles Treaty and to believe that Wilson was "bankrupt morally." The poorly edited article has several misplaced paragraphs.

080. DeWitt, Howard A. "The 'New' Harding and American Foreign Policy: Warren G. Harding, Hiram W. Johnson, and Pragmatic Diplomacy." Ohio History, 86 (Spring 1977), 96-114.

DeWitt argues that in his political relationships with Johnson, "Harding demonstrated a conciliatory style which defused the potential criticism of the isolationists." Although he thought of Johnson as radical, Harding stated that he considered Johnson to be the official party spokesman on foreign policy in an attempt to induce Johnson to campaign for him. Johnson did so, but in a

"lackluster and uninspiring manner." As president,
Harding created a Republican consensus on foreign policy
"that rendered Johnson's criticism ineffective."

081. Fleming, Denna F. The United States and the League of
Nations:  1918-1920. New York: Russell & Russell, 1968, pp.
212, 341, 454, 467, 559.

This is, perhaps, the definitive treatment of the League
of Nations controversy. Though Fleming admits a mild pro-
Wilson bias, he concedes that Johnson and other antitreaty
senators "were out speaking to immense audiences and
eliciting even stronger emotions than Mr. Wilson could
stir." Johnson was so successful, some felt he was
running away with the 1920 Republican presidential
nomination and so called him back to Washington. Fleming
concludes that "it was the Irreconcilables who really won
the post war struggle in the United States. This band of
a dozen determined and ruthless Senators . . . dominated
the conflict at almost every stage."

082.  Lodge, Henry Cabot.  The Senate and the League of
Nations.  New York: Charles Scribner's Sons, 1925, pp. 102,
103, 120, 151, 190, 194, 297, 306, 322, 325, 329, 330, 335-
345, 372, 376, 378.

The most interesting aspect of the Senate majority
leader's account of how the Senate handled the League of
Nation's Treaty is its verbatim report of a conference at
the White House between Wilson and members of the Senate,
including Johnson. Johnson raised a number of questions
related to Article Ten and to the secret treaties which
disposed of territories belonging to belligerents.

083. Lower, Richard Coke. "Hiram Johnson: The Making of an
Irreconcilable." Pacific Historical Review, 41 (November
1972), 505-526.

Partisan politics and ambition "played almost no part in
shaping the Senator's ideas" about the League of Nations.
Johnson believed that American involvement in the war had
postponed progressive advances at home and membership in
the league would lead to further foreign adventures. The
Russian intervention was an example of what was to come.
America's postwar responsibilities must be limited to our
own "backyards." Article Ten would keep America
perpetually involved against the forces of change.

084. McKenna, Marion C. Borah. Ann Arbor: University of
Michigan Press, 1961, pp. 88, 134-135, 138, 157, 159, 161-
162, 168-170, 172-173, 179, 181, 189, 218, 228, 232, 245-246,
344.

Johnson and Borah worked together on a number of foreign
policy issues. They opposed the League of Nations, often

appearing together at the same rally.  They fought the
Four Power Treaty in 1922 and defeated the World Court
protocol in 1933.  They shared progressive ideals, and in
1920 Borah led Johnson's unsuccessful bid for the
Republican presidential nomination.

085.  Maddox, Robert James.  William E. Borah and American
Foreign Policy.  Baton Rouge: Louisiana State University
Press, 1969, pp. 41-42, 44, 46, 64-65, 77-83, 133, 143, 146,
151, 153, 155, 157, 226, 243, 245.

Johnson and Borah joined efforts to force Wilson to
withdraw American troops from Russia in the winter of
1918-1919.  Together they dictated strategy to Henry Cabot
Lodge in the League of Nations struggle.  Borah offered
strong support for Johnson's attempt to win the Republican
presidential nomination in 1920, though Maddox describes
Johnson as "impetuous, eccentric, inclined toward
demagogy."  Both Johnson and Borah attempted to get
Harding to state unequivocally his position on the League
of Nations but with little success.  Together they spoke
for neutral rights (1935-39) but failed to prevent the
repeal of the arms embargo in 1939.

086.  Morison, Elting E. (ed.).  The Letters of Theodore
Roosevelt.  Cambridge: Harvard Univ. Press, 1951, Vol. 8,
418, 487, 659, 702, 720-722, 743, 771, 781, 784, 832, 845,
894, 999, 1026, 1119, 1153, 1228, 1338.

This collection of Roosevelt's letters contains a number
of letters to Johnson as well as references to him in
letters to others.  Volumes 6 and 8 contain indexes to the
previous volumes.  Earlier volumes contain no mention of
Johnson.

087.  Older, Mrs. Fremont.  William Randolph Hearst:
American.  New York: D. Appleton-Century Co., 1936, pp. 343,
349, 352, 415, 425, 426, 484, 552.

Johnson believed that the opposition of the Hearst papers
to the League of Nations played an important role in its
defeat by the Senate.  Hearst initiated an investigation
of the Power Trust when Johnson's efforts to build Boulder
Dam seemed stymied.

088.  Paterson,  Thomas G.   "California Progressives and
Foreign Policy."  California Historical Society Quarterly, 47
(December 1968), 329-342.

Paterson uses California Progressives as a case study to
show the relationship between domestic and foreign
affairs.  California Progressives were decidedly split on
questions of foreign relations.  Johnson's positions on
intervention in Mexico and preparedness for World War I
are noted briefly.

089.  Stone, Ralph.  The Irreconcilables: The Fight Against
the League of Nations.  Lexington: University Press of
Kentucky, 1970, pp. 1, 4, 20-21, 35, 37, 40, 41, 43n, 43-44,
46, 73, 82, 84, 89, 93, 96, 98, 99, 106, 107, 108, 111, 114,
115, 123, 124-125, 128, 131-132, 140, 143, 146, 149, 152,
155, 156-157, 159, 171, 174-175, 180, 185.

Stone provides an excellent analysis and description of
the thirteen senators known as the "Irreconcilables," who
were steadfast in their opposition to United States
ratification of the Treaty of Versailles and its
involvement the League of Nations.  Included is an
excellent account of their stump speaking campaign and
other strategies employed against Wilson.  Stone reports
that "Johnson, having won the recognition of his fellow
bitter-enders as the most effective orator before large
audiences, was given the heaviest speaking burden."

090.  Vinson, John Chalmers.  Referendum for Isolation:
Defeat of Article Ten of the League of Nations Covenant.
Athens: University of Georgia Press, 1961, pp. 106, 112, 114,
119, 129.

At a critical point in the deliberations of a seven-man
bi-partisan committee to reach a compromise on the League
Treaty (especially on Article Ten) Majority Leader Lodge
was called from the meeting and told by Johnson, Borah,
and others that a compromise would end Republican party
unity.  Lodge bowed to the Irreconcilables.

091.  Weatherson, Michael A.  "Hiram W. Johnson's 'Persuade
the People Campaign,' 1919: Opposition to Wilson's League."
M.A. Thesis.  California State University, Fresno, 1976.

Johnson's stump speaking campaigns against the League of
Nations are described in detail. Weatherson compares the
arguments presented by President Woodrow Wilson during his
western tour with those presented by Johnson who trailed
the president during the campaign.  Johnson relied more on
specific examples while Wilson relied on his credibility
to persuade the populace.  Johnson demonstrated that there
was a large segment of the population who did not support
the treaty or the league.

**The Issue is America and I am an American:**
**Johnson for President**

092.  Anonymous.  "Editorial."  American Review of Reviews,
46 (May 1920), 463-465.

The editor discusses Johnson's recent primary victory in
Michigan and contrasts Johnson with Herbert Hoover who is
expected to be Johnson's biggest challenger in the May 4
California primary.

093. Anonymous.  "Election Talk," New Republic 22 (5 May 1920), 302-303.

The author notes the problem faced by any Republican candidate--how to hold the party together.  "What," he asks, "can anyone say that will please at the same time a follower of Wood and a follower of Johnson, Borah or La Follette?"  The author concludes that only Johnson or Hoover can hold the party together enough to win in November.

094. Anonymous. "Has California Eliminated Hoover?" Literary Digest, 65 (15 May 1920), 21-23.

A number of Republican newspapers are quoted to show the effect of Johnson's presidential primary victory over Herbert Hoover in California.  Some felt Hoover was finished as a viable candidate; others did not.  Johnson still had fewer than 100 pledged delegates out of the 496 needed for the presidential nomination.

095. Anonymous.  "Hiram Johnson--Problem."  New Republic, 22 (19 May 1920), 367-369.

Johnson carried Michigan, Nebraska, Montana, and California in the Republican primaries.  He did well in New Jersey and Indiana.  One reason for Johnson's good showing is his ability to pick up Democratic votes.  A number of voters oppose the League of Nations and Johnson is strong on domestic issues.  He "has a tangible record in such matters as a fair deal for labor and protection of civil liberties."

096. Anonymous.  "Hiram Johnson's American Made Radicalism." Literary Digest, 65 (3 April 1920), 51-56.

Senator Johnson's director of publicity prepared a sketch of Johnson's career and that sketch is quoted at great length here.  The sketch may be the source of the oft-repeated story of how Johnson, upon learning of Heney's being shot, agreed immediately to prosecute Boss Ruef. Johnson's first campaign for governor and his handling of the IWW army in Sacramento are two incidents offered to show Johnson's fitness for the presidency.

097. Anonymous.  "Hiram Johnson's Chances."  Literary Digest, 79 (1 December 1923), 18-19.

Johnson's campaign for the Republican presidential nomination is based on his opposition to "standpatism" and to foreign entanglements.  A list of Republican newspapers opposed to Johnson is given along with an analysis of his "waning influence" in California.  Most agree, however, that Johnson is a strong stump campaigner.

098. Anonymous.   "Hiram Johnson's Chances in his Own State."
Literary Digest, 80 (26 January 1924), 5-7.

The Literary Digest polled newspaper editors in California
to determine whether or not they supported Johnson against
Coolidge in the presidential primary.   They found the
editors two to one in favor of Coolidge.   Republican
editors are quoted to show sentiment for and against
Johnson.

099. Anonymous.   "Hiram Johnson's Platform." The Outlook 136
(16 January 1924),   85-86.

An editorial writer analyzes Johnson's speech of January
3, 1924, in which Johnson entered the race for the
Republican nomination for president.   Johnson's claim that
southern delegates had too much control over the
Republican nomination process is accepted.   The writer
rejects Johnson's arguments against a tax reduction and in
favor of a bonus bill for veterans.

100. Anonymous.   "Johnson and the Chicago Convention."
Weekly Review, 2 (15 May 1920), 504-505.

Johnson will not be the nominee of the convention but he
will be a "vital factor" in determining the nominee and in
shaping the platform.   Johnson owes his primary victories
to the pro-Germans, pro-Irish, and pro-Russians.

101. Anonymous.   "A Letter from Johnson."   Literary Digest,
78 (8 September 1923),   11-12.

The author discusses the effect that publication of a
private letter between Johnson and C. K. McClatchy, editor
of the Sacramento Bee, will have on Johnson's presidential
hopes.   In the letter Johnson was pessimistic about his
chances in the California Republican primary and his
opponents attempted to use the letter to their advantage.
A number of newspapers are quoted to show the effect of
the letter on Johnson's candidacy.

102. Anonymous.   "Michigan's Boost for Johnson."   Literary
Digest, 65 (17 April 1920), 36.

Johnson's victory over Leonard Wood, a lifelong friend of
Theodore Roosevelt, in the Michigan presidential primary
shows that Johnson is TR's political heir.   Johnson beat
Wood by 40,000 votes with Herbert Hoover a poor third,
though Hoover won the Democratic primary.   Johnson's stand
against the League of Nations and his popularity with
labor in Detroit helped carry him to victory.

103. Anonymous.   "Progressivism--The Vintage of 1924." New
Republic 37 (28 November 1923), 4-6.

The author finds progressivism of 1924 significantly different from that of 1912. The programs of the new Progressives are vague because different areas of the country favor and oppose differing domestic policies.

104. Anonymous. "The Return of an Innocent Abroad." The Outlook, 134 (August 1923), 534-535.

The editor analyzes Johnson's speech of July 26, delivered in New York upon his return from Europe. Johnson warned that we were not so superior to Europeans that we could solve Europe's problems that Europeans had been unable to solve. He also spoke against U.S. involvement in the World Court which he believed could not fulfill its supporters' hopes for it.

105. Anonymous. "Sombreros in the Ring." The Freeman, 8 (12 December 1923), 316-317.

A "long career of political compromise" has stilled Johnson's progressive call and he seems content to offer "decorous generalizations" about domestic issues. Even if he gains popular support throughout the primaries, the final decision on the Republican candidate will be made by a "little group of anonymities."

106. Anonymous. "The Southern Delegate 'Scandal.'" Literary Digest, 80 (5 January 1924), 14-15.

Johnson considers a measure increasing southern representation in the Republican National Convention to be "repugnant to every sense of fair dealing." States which have never voted Republican are treated equally with those which have always supported Republican candidates.

107. Anonymous. "What Johnson Would Do as President." Literary Digest, 79 (22 December 1923), 8-9.

Johnson's "opening gun" in the campaign for president in 1924 was a speech in Chicago in which he favored a reduction in taxes, a bonus for soldiers, lower freight rates, adequate child labor laws, a minimum wage for women, and no entangling foreign alliances. Editorial comments from a number of newspapers are offered. Most are unfavorable, especially on the supposed contradiction of offering a bonus and a tax reduction at the same time.

108. Austin, Mary. "Hoover and Johnson: West Is West." The Nation 110 (15 May 1920), 642-644.

Austin compares Hiram Johnson and Herbert Hoover as potential presidents. A number of Johnson's accomplishments as governor of California are listed. Austin disputes the notion of "Big Business" that Hoover would be a "safer" candidate.

109.    Bagby,    Wesley M.    The Road to Normalcy: The
Presidential Campaign and Election of 1920.    Baltimore: Johns
Hopkins University Press, 1968 (3rd printing), pp. 16, 23,
31-40, 45, 48-53, 79-86, 92-100, 135-140, 150, 158, 166.

According to Bagby, the 1920 election was "decisive"
because it marked the lessening of support for the
progressive movement and for America's entry into foreign
affairs.    Johnson's primary campaign is described.
Johnson won 112 instructed delegates and 965,651 popular
votes, but he was not acceptable to the politicians who
ran the Republican convention.    Other candidates sought
Johnson as their running-mate but he rejected vice
presidency offers from Wood, Lowden, and Harding.

110.    Bagby, Wesley M.    "The 'Smoke Filled Room' and the
Nomination of Warren G. Harding," Mississippi Valley
Historical Review, 41 (March 1955), 657-674.

The role of the smoke filled room in the Republican
convention of 1920 has been exaggerated.    A number of
forces were at work to insure the nomination of Harding.
Although Johnson started with the third highest number of
delegates the majority were utterly "out of sympathy with
him."    Both Wood and Harding offered Johnson the vice
presidential nomination for his support.

111. Baldwin, Elbert F.    "Hiram Johnson:    His Assets and
Liabilities."    The Outlook, 124 (21 April 1920), 696-698.

Johnson's personality, his record as governor, his
activities as senator, and his qualifications for the
presidency are described.    Johnson's strength of
character" and "aggressive earnestness" as well as his
speaking ability are seen as his greatest strengths.    His
main weakness is his lack of vision on international
questions.

112.    Batman, Richard Dale.    "The Road to the Presidency:
Hoover, Johnson, and the California Republican Party, 1920-
1924.    Ph.D. Thesis.    University of Southern California,
1965.

Batman describes the rival campaigns of Hoover and Johnson
for the Republican presidential nomination in 1920 and
1924.    Johnson's relationship with William Randolph Hearst
and other supporters are discussed.    Batman offers reasons
for Johnson's failure to win the nomination.

113.    Best, Gary D.    "The Hoover-for-President Boom of 1920."
Mid-America, 53 (October 1971), 227-244.

Progressives were divided in 1920 between Hoover and
Johnson, polarizing between the positions of the Nation
(which supported Johnson) and the New Republic (which

favored Hoover.)  Once Hoover announced he would run as a Republican, many Californian Democrats gave their support to Johnson and large numbers crossed party lines to vote for him in the Republican primary.

114.  Burner, David. "Election of 1924." in Arthur M. Schlesinger, Jr. and Fred L. Israel (eds.). History of Presidential Elections, 1789-1986.  New York: McGraw Hill Book Co., 1971, Vol 3, 2459-2490.

In Johnson's opening campaign address (January 2, 1924 in Cleveland), he attacked the Republican National Committee for increasing the number of southern delegates to the Republican convention and criticized Coolidge for supplying arms to the government forces in Mexico.  To head off Johnson's campaign, Coolidge used his power of patronage and increased federal aid to farmers.

115.  Cullinan, Eustace.  "The Case for Hiram Johnson." The Outlook, 136 (19 March 1924), 480-481.

Both big business and labor in California support Johnson. Cullinan argues that Johnson's image as one who only attacks and destroys is inaccurate: "Eastern opponents cannot convince California that Hiram W. Johnson is merely a talker and not a doer, a destroyer and not a builder, a theorist and not a practical administrator."

116.  David, Paul T., Ralph M. Goldman, and Richard C. Bain. The Politics of National Party Conventions.  Menasha, WI: The Brookings Institution, 1960, pp. 236, 276, 395, 438, 535, 539, 543-546.

Johnson's treatment at the 1920 and 1924 Republican conventions provides a number of examples of how primary and convention systems work.  In 1920, for instance, the Oregon delegation, although legally committed to Johnson, gave him only limited support.

117.  [Gilbert, Clinton].  The Mirrors of Washington.  New York: G. P. Putnam's Sons, 1921, pp. 182-194.

Gilbert, who originally published his expose anonymously, paints a negative picture of Johnson as an ambitious politician with little concern for the public whom he represents.  Johnson, the author writes, "has no political philosophy.  He has no real convictions.  He does not reason or think deeply.  His mentality is slight.  He is the voice of many; instinctively he gives tongue to what the many feel; that is all."

118.  Hard, William. "How Many Hirams?" The Nation, 117 (12 December 1923), 685-686.

Hard answers the question "Has Johnson changed?" with a

"no." He is still the same man elected in 1917. He is still a Progressive on a number of domestic issues from labor laws protecting women to keeping large corporations out of politics. On economic issues, he is his own man, favoring restrictive tariffs to aid California's agriculture and federal aid for merchant marines.

119. Hard, William. "Johnson Chases Coolidge." The Nation, 118 (16 January 1924), 59.

Johnson found it difficult to campaign against Calvin Coolidge since Coolidge made few public pronouncements on important issues. Coolidge, however, kept in close contact with public officials and politicians in the Republican party through personal letters and interviews. Coolidge's attitude toward a bonus for veterans and his endorsement of the Mellon tax plan indicated to Johnson that Coolidge favored the rich over the poor, but he was hard pressed to make significant issues out of them.

120. Hard, William. "Johnson for President." New Republic, 21 (25 February 1920), 382-385.

A letter to the editor argues that Johnson deserves as much consideration for the presidency as Hoover. Quotations from Johnson's speeches are offered to show his position on the issues, especially against the League of Nations.

121. Hennings, Robert E. "Harold Ickes and Hiram Johnson in the Presidential Primary of 1924" in Donald F. Tingley, (ed.). Essays in Illinois History: In Honor of Glenn Huron Seymour. Carbondale: Southern Illinois University Press, 1968, pp. 101-119.

Johnson's defeat in the Illinois Republican primary of 1924 "ended all pretense that he was a serious candidate." Lack of money, a weak organizational structure, a late start, and the publicity given previous primary losses all contributed to Johnson's defeat. Johnson's inability to find a compelling domestic issue resulted in little press coverage of his campaign.

122. Hutchinson, William T. Lowden of Illinois: The Life of Frank O. Lowden. Chicago: University of Chicago Press, 1957. 2 Volumes. pp. 250, 394, 397-98, 419, 422-23, 427, 430, 438-440, 442, 444, 447-450, 452-54, 456, 459-462, 465, 533, 562.

Opposition to the League of Nations was the cornerstone of Johnson's presidential candidacy in 1920 and cost him the support of many Republicans. Illinois Governor Frank Lowden polled more votes than Johnson did in the South Dakota primary, but lost in Michigan and Nebraska. Hutchinson claims that the most surprising preconvention development was the "unexpected strength of Hiram

Johnson, evident wherever rank-and-file Republicans could make their preferences known." Warren Harding and Lowden agreed that they would deliver as many of their own delegates as possible to the other if it appeared Johnson or Leonard Wood might capture the nomination.

123.  Joy, Alexander C.  "Senator Johnson's Campaign." American Review of Reviews, 61 (June 1920), 603-606.

Joy describes how Johnson's 1920 presidential primary campaign had grown in the East from a one-man organization (Angus McSween) to the point where "I'm for Hiram" buttons were seen everywhere.  Much of Johnson's success was due to his campaign oratory.  According to Joy, "He can grip an audience for two hours, holding attention as few men in public life can hold it."

124.  Landfield, Jerome.  "Hiram W. Johnson in Fact and Fancy."  Weekly Review, 2 (22 May 1920), 537-540.

Landfield's purpose is to examine Johnson's career in California "objectively" in order to determine if his accomplishments and character justify his popular reputation.  Landfield contends that the Southern Pacific had been out of politics before Johnson started to campaign against it.  Johnson remained silent on the vote for women issue.  Once in the governor's office, Johnson exercised more complete control than Tammany.  Hughes lost California because Johnson knew Hughes would be his greatest rival for the nomination four years later.

125.  Lief, Alfred.  Democracy's Norris.  New York: Stackpole Sons, 1939, pp. 198, 205, 207, 217, 222, 266, 273, 299, 321, 324, 349, 400, 403, 452.

Norris and Johnson fought together in the Senate for war profit taxes.  Norris supported Johnson for president in 1920.  He believed that if a national presidential primary had been held, Johnson would have won the Republican nomination by a landslide.  Norris and Johnson supported FDR against Hoover in 1932.

126.  Lowry, Edward.  Washington Close-ups: Intimate Views of Some Public Figures.  Boston: Houghton Mifflin Co., 1921, pp. 49-60.

Lowry describes Johnson as a major political figure and compares him to other great leaders in the nation:  "Both Johnson and Bryan derive whatever power and authority they possess directly from the electors without the aid of any intermediaries or organization. . . . Mr. Johnson is a herald with a trumpet. He is militant. He summons to arms. He blows a blast outside the walls of Jericho, and if the walls do not fall he uses a battering-ram. Like any knight errant he is always ready to tilt a joust against any one who does not measure up to his ideas of a champion of the public weal."

127. McCoy, Donald R. Calvin Coolidge: The Quiet President. New York: The MacMillan Company, 1967, pp. 112, 115-119, 239-242.

Coolidge's biographer views the Republican nominating conventions of 1920 and 1924 from the Coolidge perspective. In 1920 Coolidge found himself with much less money than Johnson, so he did not attempt to enter many state preferential primaries. He saw himself as a dark horse should Johnson, Wood, and Lowden deadlock. In 1924 Coolidge carried California in the Republican primary, thus discrediting Johnson as a serious opponent.

128. Overacker, Louise. The Presidential Primary. New York: The MacMillan Co., 1926, pp. 27, 33, 46, 52, 62, 70, 71, 73, 74, 77, 87, 88, 113, 119, 122-123, 126, 127, 153, 156-157, 163, 178, 206.

Overacker provides an excellent summary and analysis of the 1920 and 1924 presidential primary elections. In the 1920 primary campaign, for example, Leonard Wood "spent over $1.00 for every vote he polled; Johnson less that $.20; or to put in another way, with a total expenditure one-fifth of Wood's Johnson polled one and one-third times as many votes." In addition, Overacker discusses the problem with the primary laws in various states, such as in North Carolina where "Johnson was the choice of the primary" but only one delegate voted for him on the first ballot.

129. Owens, John W. "Hiram Johnson at Large Again." New Republic, 26 (May 1921), 378-379.

Owens declares Johnson's speech on the Columbian treaty to be "by far the most interesting of all made in the debate. . . ." Johnson, "on fire with longing for the Presidency," must appeal to the popular mind over heads of the party leaders. Johnson's beliefs are precisely those of the majority of the Republican party.

130. Owens, John W. "The Tragic Hiram." American Mercury, 1 (January 1924), 57-61.

Owens argues that Johnson's inability to take defeat graciously in 1920 significantly hurt his chances of receiving the Republican nomination in 1924. While other potential candidates carried on after the election, Johnson did little to remain in the public eye and alienated potential allies with his "childish sulking."

131. Roseboom, Eugene H. A History of Presidential Elections. 3rd Edition. New York: MacMillan Co. 1970, pp.

370, 385-86, 390, 394, 397, 410, 440.

Johnson's failure to capture the Republican presidential nomination in 1920 is blamed on his lack of funds, the antipathy of practical politicians who blamed him for the defeat of Hughes in 1916 and his "irreconcilability" toward the League of Nations. At the 1924 convention, Johnson polled only 10 votes.

132. Shover, John L.  "The California Progressives and the 1924 Campaign."  California Historical Quarterly, 51 (Spring 1972),  59-74.

Johnson's stand against the League of Nations alienated him from some of his progressive allies, including Chester Rowell, and his support of Samuel Shortridge for the Republican senatorial nomination in 1920 cost him the political friendship of William Kent.  Both men supported Coolidge against Johnson in the 1924 Republican presidential primary.  Johnson won only 45.7 percent of the vote and suffered his only election defeat in California.  In the general election Johnson refused to campaign for Coolidge or La Follette, the Progressive party candidate.

133. Simonds, Frank H.  "The Candidate Who Was."  New Republic, 39 (28 May 1924),  16-17.

Simonds laments the fact that Johnson "permitted himself to be penetrated and absorbed by the enemy, became for those who followed him indistinguishable in thought and in action from those men whom he was expected to destroy." Simonds sees Johnson as a "fighter" who stopped fighting and became like those around him.

134. Swanberg, W. A.  Citizen Hearst.  New York: Charles Scribner's Sons, 1961, pp. 92, 333, 334, 336, 337, 365, 381, 473.

Warren Harding asked Hearst to invite Johnson to be Harding's running-mate in 1920.  Hearst did so, but Johnson refused.  Hearst hoped Johnson would lead a third-party effort, but Johnson was not interested.

135. Villard, Oswald Garrison.  "Hiram W. Johnson."  The Nation, 110 (5 June 1920), 748-749.

The editor of the Nation supports Johnson for the Republican nomination:  "He stands head and shoulders above most other candidates because he feels profoundly certain wrongs in our government and burns with indignation about them, as with the desire to right them." The odds are against Johnson because the "bosses have not forgiven him for 1912, but Johnson and his lieutenant, William Borah, have a "cause" and "they will lead it with a power that no other group of men will bring to the advocacy of their nominee."

136. Villard, Oswald G. "The 'Unbossed' Republican Convention." The Nation, 110 (19 June 1920), 820-821.

Johnson's candidacy at the Republican convention was handled badly. While Johnson was engrossed in the platform fight on the League of Nations treaty, there was no one to canvass delegations on his behalf. Additionally, Charles Wheeler's nominating speech drove many delegates away from Johnson.

137. Williams, Edgar. "Senator Johnson's California Victory." The Outlook, 125 (19 May 1920), 111-112.

Williams believes that no one other than Hiram Johnson would have been able to defeat Herbert Hoover in the Republican presidential primary in California. He notes that many conservative Republicans who had opposed Johnson in previous elections support him. He argues that Johnson's current popularity is an "emphatic and indignant denial of the falsehood circulated in the East that he was not loyal to Hughes in 1916."

## Coolidge and Hoover: Lean Years for Johnson

138. Anonymous. "Backstage in Washington." Outlook and Independent, 160 (January 1932), 10.

Johnson is described as "Mr. Hoover's prickliest hair shirt" because of his attacks on the president's foreign policy, especially with regard to foreign debts. No one rose to Hoover's defense after Johnson's "wicked denunciation" in a recent senate speech. Johnson was allowed to sit with the Finance Committee, although he was not a member, and to cross-examine witnesses.

139. Anonymous. "The Coolidge Chances for the Nomination." Literary Digest, 79 (22 December 1923), 3-5.

Coolidge should win the Republican presidential nomination in 1924. He defeated Johnson in the South Dakota convention by a margin of two to one. David Lawrence is quoted: ". . . defeating Hiram Johnson in an agriculture state, and in the section of the country in which it had been supposed that the President would be weakest, is regarded by Mr. Coolidge's friends as quite a feather in his cap."

140. Anonymous. "Hiram Johnson's Opening Gun." Literary Digest, 78 (4 August 1923), 16.

Johnson's speech in New York City on July 25, 1923, is

called one of his best.  He has just returned from a four
month investigation of conditions in Europe and is
convinced that "Nobody in Europe cares a rap for the
International Court.  He is expected to lead the fight
against the World Court in the Senate."

141.  Anonymous.  "Johnson's Slam at Hoover."  Literary
Digest, 111 (5 December 1931), 8.

At a press conference in Chicago, Johnson declared that
Hoover ought not to seek reelection in 1932 for the good
of the Republican party.  A number of newspaper editorials
are quoted to show that most Republicans did not take
Johnson's suggestion seriously.

142.  Arnold, Ralph.  "Laying Foundation Stones."  Historical
Society of Southern California Quarterly, 37 (1955), 99-124,
243-260,  297-319.

Arnold, a long time friend and supporter of Herbert
Hoover, provides an insider's view of California
Republican politics from 1920-1928.  Especially
interesting is Arnold's account of the unsuccessful
attempt to deny Johnson the senatorial nomination in 1922
and the successful defeat of Johnson by Coolidge in the
Republican presidential primary of 1924.  Arnold supported
Coolidge in the belief that Hoover would be Coolidge's
eventual successor.

143.  Ashby, LeRoy.  The Spearless Leader:  Senator Borah and
the Progressive Movement in the 1920's.  Urbana:  Univ. of
Illinois Press, 1972,  pp. 15, 17, 19-20, 22, 24-27, 30-31,
34, 39, 48, 50, 56-57, 59, 93-95, 101-102, 109, 126, 135,
170, 174, 178, 184, 188, 191, 195, 196, 198, 205-207, 220-
221, 232-233, 248-250, 276, 282-283, 285-288, 290, 292, 294.

The inability of the Progressives in the Senate to work
together doomed their cause.  When he first entered the
Senate, Johnson felt closer to Senator William E. Borah
than to any other man, but all his endeavors to maintain a
close relationship failed.  Johnson, who envied Borah's
ability to get favorable press coverage, finally refused
to follow Borah and dubbed him "our spearless leader."

144.  Fauber, Richard E.  "The Reformer without a Cause:
Hiram Johnson, 1919-1929."  M.A. Thesis.  University of
California, Berkeley, 1960.

Johnson's major contributions during the 1920s was his
advocacy of the Boulder Dam project.  He needed "all the
political talent which he had previously manifested" to
overcome determined opposition to the bill.  Compromises
strengthened his own position rather than those of his
opponents.

145. Havenner, F. R.   "In Support of Hiram Johnson."   The Nation, 115 (16 August 1922), 166-167.

Havenner, Johnson's private secretary for many years, responds to West's charges.(154)  Johnson did not support Shortridge.  He did not favor any candidate in the Republican primary.  Kent and Johnson have political differences.  Kent is "virtually a free trader" while Johnson led the efforts for high protective tariffs for California agriculture.  Johnson has not lost many of his former political friends.  Kent has aligned himself with conservative forces in order to defeat Johnson.  Johnson's telegram to The Nation in which he calls West's article, "a nasty, untrue and malicious attack" is also printed.

146. Hicks, John D.  Republican Ascendency, 1921-1933.  New York: Harper and Row, 1960, pp. 25, 56, 86, 90, 126, 131, 136, 152, 234, 243.

Johnson did not play a significant role in political life during these twelve years.  His greatest accomplishment was the Boulder Dam bill which he guided through the Senate.  He fought for high protective tariffs for California fruit and nuts and opposed the limitations of naval forces by the London Naval Conference (1930).

147.  Hoover, Herbert.  The Memoirs of Herbert Hoover:  The Cabinet and the Presidency, 1920-1933.  New York: The MacMillan Co., 1952, pp. 11, 34-35, 36, 51, 56, 117, 229, 337,

Hoover characterizes Johnson's amendment to repudiate ratification of the seven state compact over water distribution until Congress had approved the Boulder Dam as "useless and demagogic."  Hoover claims to have rewritten Johnson's bill authorizing the dam because it was in "such socialist terms that it could not pass Congress."

148.  Knappen, Theodore M.   "The West at Washington." Sunset, 58 (June 1927), 49.

Knappen examines Johnson's claim that he is no longer infected by the sting of the presidential bee and remains skeptical.  He also describes the large number of bills which Johnson supported that aided the economy and special interests of California.

149.  Lowitt, Richard.  George W. Norris: The Persistence of a Progressive, 1913-1933.  Urbana: Univ. of Illinois Press, 1971, pp. 1, 86, 103, 133-34, 219, 230, 232, 234, 265, 351, 354, 363-64, 401, 402, 408, 413, 462, 474, 518, 539, 551, 553, 560, 561.

Johnson and Norris were close friends in the 1920s.  They

often supported each other in the Senate and Norris campaigned for Johnson in the 1920 Republican presidential primaries in Nebraska, Indiana, and New Jersey. Norris aided Johnson in his fight for the Boulder Dam project.

150. Posner, Russell M. "The Progressive Voters League, 1923-26." California Historical Society Quarterly, 36 (1957), 251-261.

Conservative Republican Friend W. Richardson captured the California governorship in 1922 and discharged or pressured out of office a number of department heads who had been appointed by Johnson. In reaction, the Progressive Voters League was formed. It contained both pro and anti-Johnson Progressives, but Johnson campaigned for its candidates, and during its three years of existence the League accomplished its purpose of restoring Progressives to elective office in California.

151. Schwartz, Jordan A. The Interregnum of Despair: Hoover, Congress, and the Depression. Urbana: Univ. of Illinois Press, 1970, pp. 9, 19, 26, 33, 47, 81, 87, 94, 101, 104, 122, 133, 157, 158, 165, 168, 173, 175, 193, 200, 217, 218, 227.

Johnson was a trenchant observer of the Senate's efforts to come to grips with the depression. Schwartz quotes his views on the Senate as a whole and on individual senators such as Arthur H. Vandenberg (a "Hoover sycophant") and Huey Long ("a wholly blaviating blatherskite").

152. Vinson, J. Chalmers. "The Parchment Peace: The Senate Defense of the Four Power Treaty of the Washington Conference." Mississippi Valley Historical Review, 39 (1952), 303-314.

All the Republicans in the Senate, except for Johnson, Borah, and La Follette voted for the Four Power Treaty in 1922. The agreement between the United States, France, Great Britain, and Japan called for the signatories to respect each other's possessions in the Pacific and to settle any controversy by conference, if regular diplomatic channels broke down.

153. Vinson, John Chalmers, William E. Borah and the Outlawry of War. Athens: Univ. of Georgia Press, 1957, pp. 31-33, 38, 42-43, 55, 80, 83-84, 86, 173.

By threatening to split the Republican party, Johnson and Borah pressured Warren Harding to avoid any proposals linked to international cooperation. Johnson accused Borah of apostasy in 1922 when Borah offered a resolution calling upon the president to summon a conference of nations to discuss world trade and financial conditions. Johnson also disagreed with Borah on the merits of outlawing war which Borah supported and Johnson opposed.

154.  West, George P.  "Hiram Johnson After Twelve Years."
The Nation, 115 (9 August 1922), 142-144.

Hiram Johnson has deserted his old liberal friends and is
working with those (e.g. M. H. De Young, editor of the San
Francisco Chronicle) he use to condemn.  Johnson supported
Samuel Shortridge ("a legal servant of the rich") against
William Kent ("a true progressive") in a recent Republican
senatorial nomination race.  Johnson has refused to take a
stand on the water and power concerns in California
because of his friends in the industry.  Upton Sinclair,
the Socialist, would be a better choice for a Progressive
voter.

155.  Zieger, Robert H.  Republicans and Labor: 1919-1929.
Lexington: University of Kentucky Press, 1969, pp. 30, 51,
179, 254, 262.

Friendly toward organized labor, Johnson showed concern
over the 1927-28 bituminous coal strike and criticized
Taft's appointment to the Supreme Court because of the
number of industrial disputes the Court would be called
upon to decide.

156.  Zinn, Howard.  La Guardia in Congress.  Ithaca, NY:
Cornell University Press, 1959, pp. 59, 64, 148.

Johnson supported the candidacy of Fiorello La Guardia for
Congress from the Twentieth District of New York in 1922.
In February 1928 Johnson introduced a resolution in the
Senate calling for an investigation of the Pennsylvania
coal mining strike while La Guardia did the same in the
House.

## FDR, The New Deal, and Neutrality:   The Final Years

157.  Anonymous.  Congressional Record Appendix,  78th
Congress, 1st session, 10 November 1943, pp. A4768-A4769.

Representative J. W. Fulbright placed in the Record an
editorial from the Arkansas Gazette of November 7, 1943.
The writer notes Johnson's "God bless America" statement
of November 5 and claims that "history might have been
vastly different if the voice of America" had spoken in
meetings of the League of Nations.  Johnson's refusal to
cooperate with foreign nations is compared to the citizen
who refuses to maintain police, fire, and health services
for his community.

158.  Anonymous.  "Flynn's Big Job."  Newsweek, 16 (12 August
1942), 13.

When FDR said he didn't think anyone thought of Johnson as
a Progressive or a liberal, Burton K. Wheeler responded
that he thought Johnson was "one of the great liberals of
the country." Johnson sarcastically noted that he would
still be considered a liberal by the president if he had
gone along with "his attempted packing of the Supreme
Court. . . ."

159. Anonymous. "Headliner: Johnson--'Ye Peoples' Roaring
Senator from California." Newsweek, 5 (26 January 1935), 15.

The author describes a number of Johnson's speaking and
personal characteristics: "Senator Johnson enjoys both
fighting and hating. He always has. . . . he remains one
of the least popular Senators. He is a good worker but a
poor mixer. . . . Lack of exercise has given the Senator
plenty of paunch."

160. Anonymous.  "Johnson's Foreign Bond Show Wins Applause
but Misses Point." Business Week, 3 February 1932, pp. 26-
27.

Johnson's attack on international bankers has gained him
favorable publicity but has done nothing constructive.
Warning Americans against investing in foreign bonds is
unnecessary.  Johnson's real motive is to embarrass
Secretary of State Stimson and to demonstrate what happens
whenever the U.S. enters into foreign entanglements.

161. Anonymous. Memorial Services of Hiram Warren Johnson.
Washington: U.S. Government Printing Office, 1948.

This transcript of the memorial services for Johnson in
the House and Senate on May 28, 1946, contains a number of
addresses and tributes to Johnson, including those of
Senators William Knowland and Sheridan Downey, and
Representative Franck Havenner who followed Johnson's
career as a newspaper reporter and later served as his
private secretary.

162. Anonymous.  "Peace Passion Cold." Time, 27 (24
February 1936), 15-16.

Time credits Johnson's work in the Senate Foreign Affairs
Committee with killing the hopes for a permanent
neutrality act.  The Senate knew that "Hiram Johnson was
once more on the warpath."

163. Baker, Leonard. Back to Back: The Duel Between FDR and
the Supreme Court. New York: The MacMillan Co., 1967, pp.
138-139, 142, 272-273.

Baker considers Johnson a giant of American politics and
notes that until FDR's time, the Senate was the only
creative forum of the federal government.  Baker believes

that fear and jealousy of FDR's growing power led many otherwise liberal senators to oppose his bill reorganizing the Supreme Court.

164.  Boyle, Peter G.  "The Roots of Isolationism: A Case Study."  Journal of American Studies, 6 (April 1972), 41-50.

Boyle offers Johnson as a "useful test case" to widen our knowledge of American isolationism.  Johnson's position "had a not unreasonable logical basis."  Forces influencing Johnson toward isolationism were his progressive views, the "geographical insularity of the environment of his early life," and certain personality traits.  Party connection and ethnic origin had little influence.  Most important in Johnson's case was "his application to the 1930s of ideas formulated in the circumstances of a generation in the past."

165.  Burke, Robert E.  "Election of 1940."  In Arthur M. Schlesinger, Jr. and Fred L. Israel, (eds.).  History of Presidential Elections, 1789-1968.  Vol. 4.  New York: McGraw Hill Book Company, 1971, 2917-2946.

In September 1939, Johnson led the "peace bloc" against Roosevelt's plan to repeal or modify the embargo provision of the Neutrality Act of 1937.  He had strong support from Vandenberg (Michigan), Nye (North Dakota), La Follette, Jr. (Wisconsin), Wheeler (Montana), and Clark (Missouri), but Roosevelt's proposal was adopted.  Willkie endorsed Johnson for reelection to the Senate in 1940.

166.  Cain, Earl.  "Hiram Johnson--Orator of Isolationism." Southern Speech Journal  24 (Winter 1958), 94-104.

The purpose of this article is "to trace, through decisive events of the Second World War, the extent to which Johnson announced his isolationist convictions, and to delineate the pattern of argument which he used to defend what had become a minority position."

167.  Carlson, Oliver and Ernest Bates.  Hearst: Lord of San Simeon.  New York: Viking Press, 1937, pp. 61, 222, 245, 247.

In 1927, Johnson was appointed to a special investigating committee of the Senate to determine the authenticity of documents published in the Hearst papers that the Mexican government had bribed four United States Senators (Borah, Heffin, Norris, and La Follette).  The documents were found to be transparent forgeries.  Hearst supported Johnson from 1920 to 1934, but broke with him over Johnson's vote to increase the personal income tax.

168.  Cole, Wayne S.  Roosevelt and the Isolationists, 1932-45.  Lincoln: University of Nebraska Press, 1983.  Many references with an excellent index.

Johnson played "the largest active role in isolationist and congressional responses to the war debt controversy" in the early 1930s.  Cole explores Johnson's relationship with FDR and early New Deal legislation, and discusses Johnson's fight against the court-packing scheme and changes in neutrality legislation.  Cole describes Johnson "as independent, chauvinistic, and isolationist as Borah," but "more crusty, abrasive, and subjective."  Johnson "could be a formidable political opponent, and he commanded impressive oratorical and legislative skills."

169.  Colegrove, Kenneth W.  The American Senate and World Peace.  New York: The Vanguard Press, 1944, pp. 26, 81, 86, 122, 125, 126, 127, 130, 146, 205.

Colegrove offers a negative opinion of Johnson and other isolationist senators, blaming them for many of the problems which led to World War II.  He writes that the "majority of the opponents of the League were guided by three other incentives: (1) partisanship; (2) personal bias and emotional reaction toward the President [Wilson]; and (3) senatorial jealously of its constitutional prerogatives."  Colegrove argues against the present process of ratification which requires a two-thirds majority in the Senate.  Included in the appendix is Johnson's senatorial voting record regarding measures aimed at stopping Hitler.

170.  Dallek, Robert.  Franklin D. Roosevelt and American Foreign Policy, 1932-1945.  New York: Oxford University Press, 1979, pp. 70, 71, 74, 95, 115, 118-120, 140, 181-182, 187, 190, 248, 291.

Throughout the 1930's Johnson played an important role in the Senate debates over neutrality legislation, war debts, and the World Court.

171.  DeWitt, Howard A.  "Hiram Johnson and Early New Deal Diplomacy, 1933-1934."  California Historical Quarterly, 53 (Winter 1974), 377-386.

Offered as a case study of the isolationist mind in the decade prior to WWII, DeWitt examines the economic reasons offered by Johnson for promoting isolationism.  Johnson believed that: "economic ties dictate political action," so he attempted through the Johnson Act and through strict arms embargo to avoid any entanglements between the United States and foreign nations.

172.  Divine, Robert A.  The Illusion of Neutrality.  Chicago: University of Chicago Press, 1962, pp. 52-55, 101, 106, 122, 140, 142-143, 146-148, 155, 159, 178, 185-186, 251, 258, 260, 277, 300, 313, 321, 330.

In tracing the history of neutrality legislation in the

1930s, Divine shows the effect of Johnson's opposition to "cash and carry," to the munitions control bill, to trade quotas, and to repeal of the arms embargo. Johnson's senate office was the meeting place for the strongest opponents of FDR's foreign policy initiatives.

173. Divine, Robert A. The Reluctant Belligerent: American Entry into World War II. New York: John Wiley and Sons, 1965, pp. 6-8, 36-37.

Johnson and Borah dominated the Senate Foreign Relations Committee in the early 1930s. When Johnson attempted to amend an arms embargo bill to apply impartially to all belligerents, FDR first agreed and then, at Cordell Hull's urging, killed the entire bill. Johnson opposed the "cash and carry" principle declaring that the United States should not "sell goods and then hide."

174. Feinman, Ronald L. "The Progressive Republican Senate Bloc and the Presidential Election of 1932." Mid-America, 59 (April-July 1977), 73-91.

For eight months in 1931, Harold Ickes attempted to persuade Johnson to enter Republican primary races against President Hoover, but Johnson adamantly refused. Even promised financial support from Robert McCormick of the Chicago Tribune would not entice Johnson to enter the Illinois primary. Johnson eventually endorsed and campaigned for Franklin Roosevelt, the Democratic opponent of Hoover.

175. Feinman, Ronald L. Twilight of Progressivism: The Western Republican Senators and the New Deal. Baltimore: Johns Hopkins University Press, 1981. Many references with an excellent index.

Heavily indebted to Johnson's correspondence with his family, Feinman traces how the Progressives in the Senate reacted to the domestic and foreign policies of the New Deal and explores their relationship with Franklin Roosevelt. Feinman believes that personality, as well as politics and principle, played an important role in how Johnson and his fellow Progressives responded. This is probably the most detailed account of Johnson's senatorial activities from 1930-1945.

176. Fleming, Denna Frank. The United States and the World Court. Garden City: Doubleday, Doran & Co., 1945, pp. 33, 98, 113, 119, 122-123, 159, 175.

Fleming is critical of the Senate's power to ratify treaties. The handling of the World Court issue was a "tragedy." Johnson's speech of January 13, 1934 exemplifies "the inverted oratory which was to sweep all before it. . ." Isolationist leaders took the defeatist position that union for peace would result in war.

177. Freidel, Frank. Franklin D. Roosevelt: Launching the New Deal. Boston: Little, Brown and Company, 1973, pp. 48, 55-57, 67, 144-145, 153-155, 206, 233, 253, 266, 332, 349-350, 358, 437, 444, 452-453, 456, 458, 461.

Freidel covers the Roosevelt Administration from 1932-1934. Johnson and FDR cooperated on a number of issues during the first two years of the New Deal. Johnson remained loyal to the president and was a frequent visitor to the White House.

178. Freidel, Frank. Franklin D. Roosevelt: The Triumph. Boston: Little, Brown and Company, 1956, pp. 353-356.

In this third volume of a four-volume work on Roosevelt, Freidel covers the period from 1929-1932. Roosevelt courted Johnson during the 1932 campaign. He spoke highly of him on a trip to Sacramento, and Johnson predicted his victory in California.

179. Greenbaum, Fred. "Hiram Johnson and the New Deal." The Pacific Historian, 18 (Fall 1974), 20-35.

Based on the Congressional Record and Johnson's correspondence, Greenbaum provides an excellent account of how Johnson's admiration for FDR gradually shifted to complete disillusionment between 1932 and 1939. A month before Pearl Harbor Johnson warned that FDR was leading the country into war by deceit and subterfuge.

180. Hamilton, Marty. "Bull Moose Plays an Encore: Hiram Johnson and the Presidential Campaign of 1932." California Historical Society Quarterly, 41 (September 1962), 211-221.

Hamilton's purpose is to provide a narrative of Johnson's activities in the presidential campaign of 1932 and to explain his decision to support FDR over Hoover. Johnson bolted the Republican party "not only because of his dislike for Hoover but mainly because he saw in Roosevelt a candidate with whom he could unite for a cause akin to the reform movement in California." Johnson turned down Roosevelt's offer of the interior secretaryship.

181. Havenner, Franck R. Congressional Record Appendix, 79th Congress, 1st session, 10 September 1945, p. A3811.

In his eulogy of Johnson, Representative Havenner reports on the three occasions in 1920 when presidential candidates Philander Knox, Leonard Wood, and Warren Harding asked Johnson to be their vice presidential running-mate and Johnson refused. All three men were dead before the presidential term expired. The offer by Knox to Johnson was made in Havenner's presence and Wood attempted to use Havenner as an intermediary to Johnson.

182. Hull, Cordell. The Memoirs of Cordell Hull. New York: The MacMillan Co., 1948, pp. 217, 465, 573-74.

Johnson and the other isolationists in the Senate struck Secretary of State Hull as "honest, though mistaken." Hull declares that "it took a world of patience to deal with Johnson" whom he called an "inveterate isolationist."

183. Ickes, Harold L. The Secret Diary of Harold L. Ickes. 3 Volumes. New York: Simon and Schuster, 1954, Vol I, pp. 3, 14-15, 20, 33, 42-45, 213-214, 217, 264, 285, 313, 415-416, 424-425, 532, 588, 591, 594, 693, 697-698; Vol II, 12-13, 69-70, 77, 99, 139, 191, 487, 557, 707; Vol III, 10, 284, 331, 354-355, 652-653, 664, 666.

While serving as secretary of interior, Ickes kept a detailed diary (1933-1941) of his experiences. At first Johnson and Ickes were quite close. Johnson supported FDR's programs and Ickes often visited with the Johnsons at their Washington home. The two grew apart as Johnson attacked more and more of Roosevelt's domestic and foreign policies. The diary contains both personal and political references to Johnson and to his wife.

184. Johnson, Donald Bruce. The Republican Party and Wendell Willkie. Urbana: University of Illinois Press, 1960, pp. 12, 34, 137, 151, 158, 166, 179, 183.

Mindful of what had happened to Hughes in 1916, Willkie was quick to praise Johnson throughout his 1940 campaign in California. Johnson supported Willkie because he opposed a third term for any president, even Roosevelt whom he had previously supported.

185. Jonas, Manfred. Isolationism In America, 1935-1941. Ithaca, NY: Cornell Univ. Press, 1966, pp. 18, 42-45, 47-52, 55, 57, 59, 70, 181, 245, 257, 271.

Jonas describes Johnson as a "man of stubbornly independent mind whose support was worth having and whose opposition was much to be feared." He compares Johnson's attitude toward foreign relations with that of Borah and finds differences, though the world situation tended to emphasize the similarities.

186. Lawrence, David. "Johnson Defended as Liberal..." Congressional Record, 76th Congress, 3rd session, 8 August 1940, p. 10069.

Senator Davis inserted into the Record Lawrence's Washington Evening Star article in which he argues that Johnson "is the greatest liberal in American public life today." Lawrence disagrees with Johnson over foreign

policy, especially the Johnson Act, but concludes that
Johnson "is one of those watchdogs of human liberty, who
can be counted on to put aside the plaudits of the moment
for what he believes in the long run is for the best
interests of his country."

187. Leuchtenburg, William E.    "Franklin D. Roosevelt's
Supreme Court 'Packing' Plan." in Harold M. Hollingsworth
and William F. Holmes, (eds.).   Essays on the New Deal.
Austin: University of Texas Press, 1969, pp. 69-115.

Johnson received hundreds of letters a day about
Roosevelt's plan to increase the number of justices on the
Supreme Court.  He felt forced by the plan into opposition
of the president whom he decided was devious and sought
too much power for the executive branch.

188.  Lowitt, Richard.  George W. Norris: The Triumph of a
Progressive.  Urbana: Univ. of Illinois Press, 1978, pp. 121,
142, 169, 178, 213, 259, 323, 330,

Johnson and Norris often lunched together in the Senate
dining room at the "progressive" table.  Norris supported
Roosevelt's plan to reorganize the Supreme Court while
Johnson vigorously opposed it.  Johnson called Norris a
"doddering old man" when Norris toured California speaking
for FDR against Willkie in 1940.  Johnson provided
arguments for Republicans to counter Norris whom he felt
continued to support FDR only because of Roosevelt's
support of the Tennessee Valley Authority.

189.  Moley, Raymond.  After Seven Years.  New York: Harper
and Bros., 1939, pp. 57, 58, 125-27, 154, 164, 218, 287.

Moley felt "ecstatic relief" when Johnson declared his
support for FDR in 1932.  Moley gave the word to Johnson
that the California based Bank of America would reopen
after the bank holiday of 1933.

190.  Moley, Raymond.  The First New Deal.  New York:
Harcourt, Brace and World, 1967, pp. xii, 73, 92-94, 97-98,
192-193, 368, 371-372, 386, 407, 518.

Johnson twice declined FDR's request to become secretary
of the interior.  He supported Harold Ickes whom FDR
nominated for the position.  Later FDR considered Johnson
for an appointment to the Supreme Court but decided
against him.  Moley wrote the glowing tribute to Johnson
in the speech FDR delivered in Sacramento during his first
campaign for the presidency.

191.  Moley, Raymond.  "Perspective: California Talks Back."
Newsweek, 16 (9 September 1940), 64.

Moley examines Willkie's chances to capture California in

the presidential election. California electors ignored
FDR's advice not to return Johnson to the Senate and they
might be favorably disposed toward Willkie if "he can make
them believe that . . . he is not overly concerned with
party labels." Speeches by Johnson on Willkie's behalf
could clinch the election for him.

192. Moley, Raymond. 27 Masters of Politics. New York:
Funk and Wagnalls Co., 1949, pp. 87-88, 93, 190, 232-241.

Written from a personal point of view, Moley recounts a
number of meetings with Johnson. He argues that the
eastern press was wrong to label Johnson as purely
isolationist. Johnson feared Europe because it was a
diversion which prevented the United States from solving
domestic problems and from dealing with the nations of the
Pacific. Moley believes that the early New Deal was the
acceptance of Johnson's reforms in California on the
federal level.

193. Nixon, Edgar (ed.). Franklin D. Roosevelt and Foreign
Affairs. 3 Vol. Cambridge, MA: Belknap Press of Harvard
Univ., 1969; Vol I, 115-17, 150, 151, 198, 212, 338, 377-381,
408, 409, 549; Vol II, 346, 356, 373-74, 376-77, 400, 429-
430; Vol III, 84, 164, 171-72, 178, 191. 276, 446-47.

This collection of FDR's letters, speeches, and excerpts
from press conferences is arranged chronologically and
offers a number of items written by and to Johnson from
Roosevelt. Johnson is occasionally mentioned in letters
to and from other correspondents of Roosevelt. All
materials concern foreign affairs during FDR's first term
(1933-37) when he and Johnson were still on good terms.

194. Vinson, J. Chal. "War Debts and Peace Legislation:
The Johnson Act of 1934." Mid-America, 50 (July 1968), 206-
222.

The Johnson Act, which embargoed lending to governments in
default on debts to the U.S. government, was the "first in
a series of neutrality laws through which Congress
virtually arrogated control of foreign policy and
dedicated it to peace." Introduced in 1932 to protect
American private investors from worthless foreign bonds,
the amended 1934 version cut off future credit to nations
defaulting on any war debts. FDR's relationship with
Johnson and with other Progressives is noted.

195. Wallen, Theodore C. "Johnson: Symbol of Extreme
Nationalism." Literary Digest, 119 (23 March 1935), 13.

Wallen discusses the "unique path across the pages of
history," that Johnson had cut. He reviews Johnson's
opposition to six presidents culminating in his victory
over American adherence to the World Court. Wallen

describes Johnson's physical appearance and his personality: "When Hiram Johnson is pleased to be genial there are few more winning men alive; and when he is pleased to be cantankerous he steps out of competition."

196.   White, Graham and John Maze.  Harold Ickes of the New Deal: His Private Life and Public Career.  Cambridge: Harvard University Press, 1985, pp. 85-89, 94-96, 98, 206.

Ickes was "indefatigable in his efforts to persuade Johnson to contest the presidency" in 1920 and in 1924. Harding's death and the rush of Republicans to support the incoming President, Calvin Coolidge, ended Johnson's hopes in 1924.  Between 1931 and 1932, Ickes again attempted to persuade Johnson to seek the presidency, but both Johnson and, especially, his wife were opposed to another attempt.

# 3

# Johnson as Writer

197.   Johnson, Hiram.   "Shall the People Really Rule?"
California Outlook, 12 (16 March 1912), 11-12.

In this revised version of a speech delivered by Johnson
in Los Angeles on March 9, he argued that the nation must
control its big business.  Speaking in behalf of Roosevelt
he declared: "The people are for Roosevelt; the
politicians are for Taft."  Roosevelt had been preaching
the progressive doctrine since 1908.  The "strong, cunning
men" behind the political puppets are the ones who have to
be dealt with and Roosevelt can do it.

198.   Johnson, Hiram.   "Why not a Dollar Draft?"   The
Independent, 91 (September 1917), 386.

Johnson called for the same enthusiasm for conscripting
the wealth of the nation to fight the war as had been
shown in the conscripting of manpower.  War profits should
be severely taxed.  England, which took 80 percent of
excess profits, provided a good example for America to
follow.

199.   Johnson, Hiram and Wesley Jones.   Senate.   Select
Committee to Investigate the Washington Railway and Electric
Co.  Street Railway Conditions in the District of Columbia.
Senate Report 176, 65th Congress, 1st session, 6 October
1917.

Johnson offered a separate opinion which blamed
Clarence P. King, the president of the railway company for
the strike and argued that collective bargaining (rather
than the individual bargaining required by King) "is
almost essential for the protection of employees."
Johnson recommended government ownership of the electric
railways in the District.

200.  Johnson, Hiram.   "What of the Nation?"   Sunset, 43
(October 1919), 15-16.

In the first of a series of twelve short articles, Johnson
discussed the commercial potential of the Pacific, the
need to publicize war profiteering, and the move toward a
League of Nations which he characterized as a "sham and a
snare."

201.  Johnson, Hiram.   "What of the Nation?"   Sunset, 43
(November 1919), 12-13.

Johnson attacked those correspondents who failed to inform
the public of what was happening at the Paris Peace
Conference.   He also criticized the way the government
handled the railroads during the war.   Finally, he
bemoaned the deaths of American soldiers in Russia, "blood
spilled in violation of the Constitution."

202.  Johnson, Hiram.   "What of the Nation?"   Sunset, 43
(December 1919), 15-16.

Johnson argued that awarding Shantung to Japan violated
the principle of self-determination.   He attacked the IWW
for engaging in mob violence: "To destroy the law by
violence destroys not only it but weakens the whole
barrier interposed by organized society for the people's
protection."

203.  Johnson, Hiram.   "What of the Nation?"   Sunset, 44
(January 1920), 23-24.

Johnson discussed class warfare; the Japanese question
("the Caucasian cannot compete with him and in those
agricultural pursuits to which he devotes himself the
Caucasian is compelled ultimately to yield."); the
reorganization of the peace-time army; and he predicted
that the League of Nations would be the main issue in the
upcoming elections.

204.  Johnson, Hiram.   "What of the Nation?"   Sunset, 44
(February 1920), 22-23.

Johnson's topics included a discussion of political
bosses; plans to draft the Republican platform before the
convention gets underway; the London economic conference;
and Johnson's own amendment to the League of Nations
treaty that provided for equal representation (5 votes)
for the United States and Great Britain.

205.  Johnson, Hiram.   "What of the Nation?"   Sunset, 44
(March 1920), 21-22.

Johnson noted that all the candidates for the Republican
nomination were running upon "the Roosevelt tradition."

He supported the right of Socialists to spread their
doctrines and he criticized the New York legislature for
suspending their Socialist members.  He supported
President Wilson's call for a referendum on the League of
Nations and called American policy in Siberia "a total
failure."

206.  Johnson, Hiram.    "What of the Nation?"   Sunset, 44
(April 1920), 17-18.

Johnson criticized Wilson's removal of Robert Lansing as
secretary of state.   The government cannot cease while the
president is ill.    Johnson believed that no presidential
candidate could support the League of Nations without
reservations and noted that even the English were no
longer pressing for more votes in the League that the U.S.
would have.

207.  Johnson, Hiram.   "What of the Nation?"   Sunset, 44 (May
1920), 21-22.

Johnson noted the change in attitude of some politicians
toward Theodore Roosevelt since his death: "Some who in
his life were cruelly unsparing, now vie with those who
loved him and long for him today, in unstinted praise."
The Senate had voted against the League of Nations but
Johnson's was not convinced it was the final vote since
the "international bankers" might try to revive it.
Johnson closed with some observations on the climate of
the Pacific coast and a humorous anecdote about James G.
Blaine.

208.  Johnson, Hiram.    "What of the Nation?"   Sunset, 44
(June 1920), 21-22.

Johnson noted "retrogression rather than progress" in the
movement toward preferential primaries.    Bosses still
controlled the conventions.    He condemned Japanese
occupation of Shantung and aggression in Siberia.    He
joined Borah in insisting that a limit be placed on
expenditures in national primary campaigns and gleefully
noted that President Lowell of Harvard finally supported
reservations to secure the League of Nations.

209.  Johnson, Hiram.    "What of the Nation?"   Sunset, 45
(July 1920), 22-23.

Johnson argued for primary laws in every state so that
"the will of the people rather than the coin of the
candidate" would be the controlling factor.    He also
argued that states which supported a party's candidate
should be rewarded with additional votes at the next party
convention.    California's delegation at the Republican
convention would be increased while southern delegations
would have less representation.    Johnson claimed that

excessive profits rather than increased labor costs accounted for higher railroad costs.

210. Johnson, Hiram. "What of the Nation?" Sunset, 45 (August 1920), 23-24.

Johnson wrote this article immediately after his defeat at the Republican convention. He described the behind-the-scenes struggle for a permanent chairman, the unsuccessful bid of the Kansas governor for the vice presidential nomination, and "a well-known United States Senator, who was acting in conjunction with New York bankers" who mistakenly entered Johnson's suite thus starting rumors about his loyalty. Johnson happily declared that the Republican platform rejected the League of Nations and did not mention reservations.

211. Johnson, Hiram. "What of the Nation?" Sunset, 45 (September 1920), 22-23.

Written at the conclusion of the Democratic convention, Johnson was more concerned about the earlier Republican gathering: "At Chicago those peculiar financial forces of New York, who believe the government belongs to them and its primal purpose is for their profit, were brazenly directing their willing puppets who, in turn, were manipulating delegations." Harding, for example, won ten percent of the vote in the Indiana primary but on the eighth ballot most Indiana delegates voted for him. A national primary law was again proposed. Johnson concluded with a tribute to William Jennings Bryan who "performs a real and a much needed service in our politics."

212. Johnson, Hiram. "New York City's Problem." The Forum, 66 (September 1921), 253-259.

Johnson claimed that the Traction Law, passed by the New York state legislature, was an example of "the destruction of the right of the people to govern themselves, of the principle of home rule." The new state-appointed Transit Commission could make terms and conditions with the city railroad companies which the city had to obey. Even the city owned subway would be controlled by the commission. Johnson suggested a remedy: "Give New York the initiative and referendum and there will be an end of legislative interference with New York City, an end of spoilation of its people."

213. Johnson, Hiram. "Why 'Irreconcilables' Keep Out of Europe, Told by Hiram Johnson." New York Times, 14 January 1923, Section 8, p. 1. See also Congressional Digest, 22 (August-September 1943), 214-217 and Congressional Record, 67th Congress, 4th session, 16 January 1923, pp. 1790-1793.

American money cannot produce European peace.  The U.S. should have nothing to do with the Reparation Commission or with other European conferences: "the isolation of America is not Europe's ruin.  It is a necessity to Europe's salvation."

214.  Johnson, Hiram.  Senate. Committee on Irrigation and Reclamation.  Boulder Canyon Reclamation Project.  Senate Report 654, 69th Congress, 1st session, 24 April 1926, pt. 1.

In this early report supporting a dam on the Colorado River, Johnson argued that: "It is a constructive improvement, not experimental, sound financially, well considered, shaped in the public interest, one the consummation of which will be a source alike of national pride and advantage."

215.  Johnson, Hiram.  "The Boulder Canyon Project."  The Annals of the American Academy of Political and Social Science, 125 (January 1928), 150-156.

The Swing-Johnson bill will result in a dam at Boulder Canyon on the Colorado river which will provide flood control and river regulation, reclamation of lands, the emancipation of American land from Mexican control by the building of the All-American canal, and provide domestic water for cities in southern California.  Government costs will be repaid through the sale of electric power.  Private power companies are opposing the project, but the public's right will prevail.

216.  Johnson, Hiram.  Senate.  Committee on Irrigation and Reclamation.  Boulder Canyon Project.  Senate Report 592, 70th Congress, 1st session, 20 March 1928, pt. 1.

Johnson's six-part report discussed: the project's purpose including a justification of the federal government's role; flood control efforts; the need for an "All-American" canal; irrigation usage; power generation; and the financial soundness of the project.

217.  Johnson, Hiram.  "Converting the Colorado River Into a National Asset."  Current History, 29 (February 1929), 786-792.

Johnson described "the greatest constructive work of this generation."  The history of the project was reviewed and its six purposes were listed: (1) flood control; (2) irrigation; (3) adequate water supply for the Imperial Valley; (4) revenue from water sale to southern California; (5) "a magnificent lake"; (6) "electric energy, which the impounding of the water will make possible, will alone afford a basis for recovery in full, with interest. . . ."

218.  Johnson, Hiram.  Senate. Commerce Committee.  Bridge
across San Francisco Bay.  Senate Report 33, 71st Congress,
1st session, 13 June 1929.

Writing for the Commerce Committee, Johnson argued that
"every public consideration, convenience, comfort, safety,
and economic growth" demanded a link between San Francisco
and Alameda county.  The proposed bridge would not
interfere with shipping or naval use of the bay.

219.  Johnson, Hiram.  Senate.  Committee on Foreign
Relations.  Limitation and Reduction of Naval Armament:
Individual Views.  Senate Report 1080, 71st Congress, 2nd
session, 30 June 1930, pt. 2.

Johnson argued that the London treaty was disadvantageous
to the U.S. and precluded an adequate national defense.
In a 20 page minority report, Johnson declared that the
treaty helped Japan and Great Britain at the expense of
the U.S.

220.  Johnson, Hiram.  "Should America Cancel Her Foreign War
Debts?: Con."  Congressional Digest, 10 (October 1931), 247.

In a press statement of August 23, 1931, Johnson argued
that international bankers were "the dominant factor not
only in American financial life today but in American
political life."  They owned the leaders of both political
parties.   Cancellation of foreign debts could cost the
American taxpayers $8 billion.  With unemployment so high
in the U.S. we should think of America before we aid
European nations.

221.  Johnson, Hiram.  Congressional Record, 74th Congress,
2nd session, 4 May 1936, pp. 6571-6573.

Johnson entered into the Record a written opinion in the
matter of the impeachment of District Judge Halsted L.
Ritter.   Ritter had been acquitted by the Senate on six
counts, but found guilty on the seventh which Johnson
called  "a sort of resume or catch all of the six."  The
crime of "misbehavior" of which Ritter was found guilty
was so vague as to be meaningless especially since it was
not shown to be willfully done with a corrupt intention.
Ritter handled 7000 cases without complaint and no lack of
public confidence in him had been shown.  Johnson's vote
of "not guilty" was justified.

222.  Johnson, Hiram.  Senate.  Committee on Foreign
Relations.  Promoting the Defense of the United States.
Senate Report 45, 77th Congress, 1st session, 17 February
1941, pt. 2.

Johnson offered a minority report on the lend-lease bill
which he found had "no real justification either in law or

in fact."   Too much authority was given to the president:
"It makes of the Chief Executive a dictator and worse, a
dictator with power to take us into wa "    The bill
transferred the war-making power from Co gress to the
president.

223.    Johnson, Hiram.    "Let's Declare Ourselves."    Scribner's
Commentator, 11 (December 1941), 93-97.

Johnson declared that it would be better to have a direct
vote on a declaration of war rather than "beclouding" the
issue by talking about freedom of the seas or repeal of
the Neutrality Act.   The U.S. was not prepared militarily
for all the commitments FDR listed in a recent speech.
Those who favored peace must unite and "face the
warmongers."

224.    Johnson,    Hiram.    Senate.    Committee on Foreign
Relations.   Authorizing Execution of Certain Obligations
under Treaties of 1903 and 1936 with Panama.   Senate Report
1720, 77th Congress, 2nd session, 30 November 1942, pt. 2.

Together with Senator Nye, Johnson offered a minority
report opposed to revisions in U.S. agreements with
Panama.   The proposals should be offered to the Senate in
treaty form (not as a joint resolution) and should provide
for settlement of all American claims on Panama by
arbitration.

225.    Johnson, Hiram.   Congressional Record Appendix, 79th
Congress, 1st session, 20 December 1945, pp. A5714-5716.

Four months after Johnson's death, Representative Daniel
Reed (New York) placed into the Record the senator's
statement against the repeal of the Johnson Act.   Johnson
reviewed the history of the act and quoted statements by
FDR in favor of it.   He concluded that "the conditions of
uncertainty, disorder, distrust, and near bankruptcy
prevailing today makes retention imperative."

226. Levine, Lawrence W.   "The 'Diary' of Hiram Johnson."
American Heritage, 20 (August 1969), 64-76.

Levine presents excerpts from 53 letters written by
Johnson to members of his family between April 6, 1917 and
November 3, 1944.   The letters cover many of the important
political events during Johnson's long tenure in the
Senate and present Johnson's candid views about a number
of well-known people and events.   Levine provides
annotations and reprints six cartoons featuring Johnson.

227. Lincoln, A.   "My Dear Friend and Champion: Letters
Between Theodore Roosevelt and Hiram Johnson in 1918."
California Historical Society Quarterly, 48 (March 1969), 19-
36.

The Johnson-Roosevelt correspondence continued in 1918 as Johnson defended Roosevelt on the floor of the Senate. Johnson and Roosevelt disliked Wilson and regarded the war effort "as a seething welter of inefficiency and confusion. Johnson disagreed with Roosevelt over his attempt to encourage the censure of Senator Robert La Follette for his opposition to America's entry into the war, but he supported Roosevelt on Panama Canal issues even after Roosevelt's death.

228.  Lincoln, A.  "My Dear Governor: Letters Exchanged by Theodore Roosevelt and Hiram Johnson." California Historical Society Quarterly, 38 (September 1959), 229-247.

The friendship between Johnson and Theodore Roosevelt began in 1910 and was strengthened in the campaign of 1912, and they exchanged letters regularly until Roosevelt's death in January 1919. Lincoln writes, "Their correspondence discloses that they had several personality traits in common, a striking resemblance in political philosophy and similar attitudes toward their opponents." Many excerpts from the letters are provided. Emphasis is given to the election campaign of 1912 and the formation of the Progressive party.

229.  Lincoln, A.  "My Dear Senator--Letters between Theodore Roosevelt and Hiram Johnson in 1917." California Historical Society Quarterly, 42 (September 1963), 221-239.

The Roosevelt-Johnson correspondence during 1917 and 1918 is concerned with America's war effort and its role in the peace to follow. It is also revealing of the personal characteristics of both men. Johnson often used Roosevelt's arguments and even his exact phraseology in Senate speeches. Johnson's attempts to aid Roosevelt's efforts to lead a volunteer regiment against Germany are detailed. When Roosevelt's request was denied, Johnson's bitterness toward Woodrow Wilson increased.

# 4

# Johnson as Speaker

230.  Congressional Record, 65th Congress, 1st session, 28 April 1917, p. 1481.

Johnson favored an amendment which allowed volunteers for the armed services to be accepted while the draft of conscripts was being prepared.  Johnson felt the volunteer system least affected the domestic relations of the country, though he accepted the draft as an emergency war measure.

231.  Congressional Record, 65th Congress, 1st session, 28 April 1917, p. 1492.

Johnson spoke in favor of permitting Theodore Roosevelt to raise a division of American troops to fight in France. He described Roosevelt as a man of "dynamic force, of ability, of virility, and of red-blooded courage, typifying the American nation."

232.  Congressional Record, 65th Congress, 1st session, 11 May 1917, pp. 2097-2100.

Johnson supported an amendment to strike out the censorship provision of the espionage bill.  He argued that during a time of stress the preservation of free speech was more important than ever.  The purpose of the proposed law was to render impossible legitimate criticism of the war effort.

233.  Congressional Record, 65th Congress, 1st session, 28 June 1917, p. 4403.

Johnson favored a bill to encourage the production and to conserve the supply of food and fuel even though it gave considerable power to the president.  The necessity of giving the president autocratic powers in time of war

exists to prevent hoarding and speculation.  No one should
be allowed to profit from the war.  Interestingly, Johnson
praised the newly named food administrator, Herbert
Hoover: "He is not alone a most distinguished American.
He is a distinguished world figure."

234.  Congressional Record, 65th Congress, 1st session, 1
August 1917, p. 5651.

Johnson favored a national prohibition amendment being
sent to the states for approval or rejection.  It was the
type of question the people of each state should decide
for themselves.  Johnson did not venture an opinion for or
against prohibition.  He also was concerned that the
women's suffrage amendment had not yet reached the Senate.
If any great number of people wanted an economic, ethical,
or moral question submitted to the voters, it should be
done.

235.  Congressional Record, 65th Congress, 1st session, 20
August 1917, pp. 6183-6186.

Johnson opposed the proposed revenue measure, believing
that certain rates were unjust since war profiteers were
not taxed enough.  He insisted that "we proceed to take
the largest share of these war profits that it is possible
to take."  England took 50 percent of war profits; under
this bill, the United States took 20 percent.

236.  Congressional Record, 65th Congress, 1st session, 1
September 1917, pp. 6492-6497.

Returning to the war profits issue, Johnson argued in
favor of his amendment of a flat levy of 73 percent on all
such profits.  How to figure war profits was a subject of
much discussion.  Johnson concluded, ". . . when the State
is endangered, every man, every woman, every child, and
all of its wealth must be taken for the defense of the
State."

237.  Congressional Record, 65th Congress, 2nd session, 19
February 1918, pp. 2311-2317.

Johnson began his speech on a bill for compensation to the
railroads for seizure by the federal government by
defending those who criticized the government in time of
war: "Inefficiency, incompetency, and worse flourish in
darkness.  Truth and publicity are the remedy and the
corrective."  Johnson favored a "fair return" to the
railroads during the period of government takeover, but he
found the proposed rates to be excessive. Johnson argued
that government ownership of the railroads offered the
best means of operating them effectively.

238.  Congressional Record, 65th Congress, 2nd session, 4 May

1918, pp. 6036-6037.

In Johnson's last (and unsuccessful) effort to persuade the Senate not to agree to the conference report on the espionage bill, he argued that such a bill bred discontent and made people timid and fearful. "Leave us," he concluded, "in this time of stress, the right to talk from our hearts honestly and loyally, even if it be in abuse of any part of the Government of the United States."

239. Congressional Record, 65th Congress, 2nd session, 13 May 1918, pp. 6410-6411.

Johnson argued that in levying the next quota in the draft, each state should be credited with the number of volunteers that had already enlisted from that state. California had a very high percentage of volunteer enlistments as compared to the other states.

240. Congressional Record, 65th Congress, 2nd session, 12 June 1918, pp. 7669-7672.

Johnson spoke out sharply against a proposed change in Senate rules that would limit the length of time an individual senator could speak on a bill. Examples of the president's treatment of General Leonard Wood (who was refused permission to go to Europe with the troops that he had trained) and recent increases in railroad rates were offered to show how the wartime emergency was being used to increase the power of the executive. The Senate must be free to debate and to caution against possible executive branch abuses.

241. Congressional Record, 65th Congress, 2nd session, 1 August 1918, pp. 9191-9192.

In a wide ranging effort Johnson discussed the possibility of a land-colonization plan for returning soldiers, government ownership of the railroads, and the "wretched" mail service to the soldiers in France. Speaking of his son in the service, Archibald, Johnson reported, "The letters which pass between us are numbered. He received one in six of mine. I received one in four of his."

242. Congressional Record, 65th Congress, 2nd session, 5 September 1918, pp. 9977-9979.

Johnson sharply criticized raids by the Department of Justice which, while looking for draft dodgers, rounded up thousands of young men in New York and New Jersey. Only a very small percentage were guilty of the offense for which they were taken into custody. Johnson spoke out because "the only place left in all this land where liberty finally may have its fight made for it, and where freedom may be protected, is right here in this body."

243. Congressional Record, 65th Congress, 3rd session, 12 December 1918, pp. 342-347.

Johnson introduced a resolution directing the secretary of state to send to the Senate "all data, documents, and information showing or bearing upon our present relations with Russia as to peace or war. . . ." In spite of eloquent words by the government saying that American troops would not be sent to Russia, the press reported "skirmishes and battles; of American soldiers fighting Russian soldiers." He accused the Creel Bureau of Information of misinforming the public and warned the nation against, "endeavoring to impose by military force upon the various peoples of the earth, the kind of government we desire for them and that they do not desire for themselves."

244. Congressional Record, 65th Congress, 3rd session, 17 January 1919, p. 1585.

In accepting the Fourteen Points, every nation agreed on "open covenants of peace, openly arrived at." The president was engaged in secret negotiations and "our only news is a communique, which we know from experience of the past four years is made merely to cover up what has been done." Johnson hoped that the United States would never become the world's policeman and that our troops would be returned as quickly as possible.

245. Congressional Record, 65th Congress, 3rd session, 21 January 1919, pp. 1797-1799.

Johnson spoke against the appropriation of $100 million to alleviate hunger in Europe. The real purpose of the bill, he claimed, was to create a market in Europe for packing house products. Johnson rejected the notion of further involvement in European affairs: "It is time for an American policy, for American business, for America's social life, for America's economic life. It is time for an American policy for American boys and American soldiers. . . . a soldier who has looked into the muzzle of a machine gun must not be compelled to look into an empty dinner pail."

246. Congressional Record, 65th Congress, 3rd session, 29 January 1919, pp. 2261-2270.

In a lengthy speech, quoting a number of passages from Woodrow Wilson's "Fourteen Points Address," Johnson questioned American policy toward Russia. He claimed that America was fighting an undeclared war against the government of Russia and was interfering with her national affairs. American boys were dying long after the armistice with Germany had been signed, and no one in the government had been willing to say why.

247.  Congressional Record, 65th Congress, 3rd session, 13 February 1919, pp. 3258-3264.

Johnson renewed his Senate resolution proposing that American soldiers should be withdrawn from Russia as soon as practicable.  Johnson drew a distinction between withdrawing 5000 "precious American lives" and aiding the cause of Bolshevism.  American troops were fighting an unconstitutional, undeclared war and should be returned to the United States.

248.  Congressional Record, 66th Congress, 1st session, 23 May 1919, pp. 157-160.

Johnson offered his reasons for the Senate asking the secretary of state to transmit the full text of the Paris peace treaty.  Since President Wilson promised "open covenants openly arrived at," the people of the United States were entitled to know exactly what the treaty said.  Fifteen days earlier the treaty had been published in Germany.  Why did the American people have to wait for it?  The Senate had received only a synopsis.

249.  Congressional Record, 66th Congress, 1st session, 2 June 1919, pp. 501-509.

Again requesting that the secretary of state send the Senate a full text of the Paris peace treaty, Johnson attacked the treaty as "born in secrecy, denied exposition, and presented to us with cynical indifference to our right of knowledge . . ."  Johnson presented a number of arguments he would reiterate over the next few years.  Article Ten, he claimed, would make the United States the world's peacekeeper and would "make the present generation decide the fate of all future generations."  The treaty made the operation of the Monroe Doctrine dependent on the members of the League rather than on the United States alone.  The United States had only 1 vote, the British Empire had 6.  The treaty made the U.S. an ally of Japan in forcing China to hand over territory to her.  The treaty allowed the meddling in the internal affairs of various states in regard to treatment of aliens and immigrants.  The Record notes "applause on the floor and in the galleries."

250.  Congressional Record, 66th Congress, 1st session, 26 September 1919, pp. 5970-5971.

Johnson announced that he was going to talk to the people of California, Colorado, Nevada, Oregon, Washington, and Utah about his proposed amendment to the League of Nations which would give the United States six votes, the same number as the British Empire had.

251.  Congressional Record, 66th Congress, 1st session, 16

October 1919, pp. 7002-7004.

The decision which allowed Japan the territorial right to Shantung was an "abominable and a detestable" one. It was a moral question which the Senate must come to grips with and Johnson favored an amendment to the peace treaty in which the United States declined to become a party to the despoiling of China.

252. Congressional Record, 66th Congress, 1st session, 23 October 1919, pp. 7355-7360.

Johnson spoke in favor of his amendment which gave the United States the same number of votes in the League of Nations as Great Britain had. Johnson claimed that it was "from the standpoint alone of our national dignity, our national prestige, our national progress, our national power, our American glory, and our American rights that I am making the appeal today. . . ."

253. Congressional Record, 66th Congress, 3rd session, 20 January 1921, pp. 1698-1699.

Johnson spoke in favor of a minimum wage law for federal employees. The bill called for $3 per day, $90 per month, $1080 per year. Part-time workers would get 37 1/2 cents per hour. Only if labor could live decently could they work efficiently, and no democracy should pay less than a living wage to its employees.

254. Congressional Record, 66th Congress, 3rd session, 2 February 1921, p. 2431.

Johnson spoke against the cloture rule, even though extended debate was preventing the vote on a tariff bill he strongly supported: "But putting all these disadvantages on the one side, our waste of time, our inefficiency, our inability at times to transact public business . . . upon the other the right finally in one forum in this world for the free and independent expression, without limit, outweighs all disadvantages of our methods and our procedure."

255. Congressional Record, 67th Congress, 1st session, 15 April 1921, pp. 305-310.

Johnson spoke against the proposed treaty with Colombia which called for payment of $25 million in reparation for the land taken for the Panama Canal. Such a payment was an admission that the United States had wronged Colombia in 1903 and now regretted the action. Johnson felt no wrong had ever been done and that no payment was necessary.

256. Congressional Record, 67th Congress, 1st session, 21

June 1921, pp. 2796-2797.

Johnson spoke in favor of his resolution calling for the Senate Committee on Education and Labor to investigate the civil strife in the coal fields of West Virginia. The law and the Constitution had been suspended in certain parts of West Virginia.   Deputy sheriffs, in the pay of mine owners, effectively enforced the law against striking mine workers.   "A state of civil war" existed.

257.  Congressional Record,  67th Congress,  1st session,  10 August 1921, pp. 4813-4814.

In a speech covering a number of topics, Johnson drew a distinction between being hostile toward the Harding administration (which he said he was not) and being opposed to specific administration measures.  He could not understand the recent payment of $32 million dollars to Great Britain for transporting American troops to Europe while Great Britain was not paying any of the interest on her debt to the United States.  He congratulated Senator Borah for his work in arranging a disarmament conference. He called it the "greatest personal victory that has been won by any United States senator since I have been a member of this body."

258.  Congressional Record,  67th Congress,  1st session,  18 October 1921, pp. 6408-6410.

Johnson spoke in favor of the ratification of the treaty with Germany.  He felt it would not entangle the United States in the "maelstrom of European controversies and wars."   Although opposed to the Treaty of Versailles, Johnson was not opposed to the a treaty with Germany reserving for the United States any rights gained by the treaty.   The treaty reflected the will of the American people.

259.  Congressional Record,  67th Congress,  2nd session,  26 January 1922, pp. 1752-1756.

Speaking to a very small number, Johnson proposed an amendment to the foreign loan adjustment act which would have allowed Congress to have the final approval over any adjustments to foreign loans.   Johnson argued that that the representatives of the people should not turn over their financial responsibilities to a presidential commission.   The recent disarmament conference was held in the open and so should financial dealings with other countries. Congress should have the final say on how the people's money was being spent.

260.  Congressional Record,  67th Congress,  2nd session,  27 February 1922, pp. 3093-3098.

Johnson spoke against a treaty which would have given
Japan title to all the former German-held islands in the
Pacific, north of the Equator.  These islands consisted of
three groups:  the Caroline Islands, the Marshall Islands,
and the Ladrones.  He claimed that Japan's only title to
the islands was through secret treaties signed with Great
Britain during World War I.  The rights of the United
States in the area were recognized by the Versailles
Treaty and no League of Nations, to which we were not a
part, had the power to give up our rights in the area.
The United States should not recognize what was done by
secret treaty before the war.

261.  Congressional Record, 67th Congress, 2nd session, 13
March 1922, pp. 3775-3784.

In words reminiscent of those he used against the League
of Nations, Johnson attacked the Four Power Agreement.  He
rejoiced that the Senate played an important role in the
ratification of every treaty and he rejected the idea of
isolationism, rather, "we ask only to live our own life in
our own way, in friendship and sympathy, with all, in
alliance with none."  Johnson was particularly upset at
the lack of information presented to the Senate with the
treaty:  "the paucity of information makes difficult, but
not impossible, accurate conclusions."  Nevertheless,
Johnson was sure that the new treaty could lead to war.
The claim had been made that one advantage of this treaty
was that it broke up the Anglo-Japanese alliance, but
Johnson saw nothing to fear in such an alliance.  Both
governments had said it was not directed against the
United States.  Johnson compared the Four Power Alliance
with Article Ten of the League of Nations treaty and had
both printed side-by-side in the Record. The treaty and
the League should be treated the same.

262.  Congressional Record, 67th Congress, 2nd session, 27
March 1922, pp. 4611-4614.

Following the vote in favor of a portion of the Four Power
Treaty, Johnson reviewed his reasons for opposing it.  It
would involve the United States in the problems of other
nations and could lead to involvement in war.  Johnson
spoke of the "problems" faced by California with regard to
the Japanese investment in agricultural lands, Japanese
immigration, and citizenship for Japanese aliens.

263.  Congressional Record, 67th Congress, 2nd session, 15
May 1922, pp. 6933-6935.

Johnson spoke in favor of a protective tariff for citrate
of lime and citric acid, both products of lemons.  Johnson
claimed that the California lemon industry was "a new
industry" which needed protection, especially from Italian
imports.  Labor costs for a pound of citric acid in the

United States were 35.6 cents; in Italy, 8.9 cents. Under present circumstances, American growers were unable to compete in the U.S. market, and "carload after carload" of lemons were being dumped.

264. Congressional Record, 67th Congress, 2nd session, 15 May 1922, pp. 6957-6958.

Johnson offered an amendment to the tariff bill raising the rate on olive oil and addressed the general question of the value of protective tariffs. He found nothing burdensome in such tariffs "when we accord these thousands who have given their all for the production of something which before we did not possess, a measure of protection which may enable them to produce and to live." Johnson compared the wages of the workers in the olive industries of Italy and Spain with those paid in the United States to show their great disparity. Even in freight rates, the U.S. grower was at a disadvantage.

265. Congressional Record, 67th Congress, 2nd session, 3 July 1922, pp. 9909-9910.

Johnson asked for protection "commensurate with the difference in the cost of production abroad and the cost of production at home" for the almond industry. He inserted in the Record various tables comparing the cost of almond production in the U.S. and overseas. On July 5, Johnson spoke similarly for the walnut industry (pp. 9963-9965).

266. Congressional Record, 67th Congress, 4th session, 29 December 1922, pp. 1046-1050.

Johnson spoke against William Borah's amendment to a naval appropriations bill which called for an international conference for the "restoration of trade and to the establishment of sound financial and business conditions." Johnson felt that such a "general omnibus endeavor . . . has neither limitations nor specifications." The futility of such a conference was shown by an extended illustration of a "great, robust, powerful creditor" who invited six debtors into his home for a conference but would do nothing to lessen the amount of debt each creditor owed him. The conference ended with all parties angry.

267. Congressional Record, 67th Congress, 4th session, 4 January 1923, pp. 1223-1224.

Johnson spoke against sending "official" representatives to the Reparation Commission. They would become "part of a sovereign power, directing, managing, operating, and conducting the affairs of the territory over which the Reparation Commission rules." Such activity could lead to military occupation of Europe if a country defaulted on its reparation payments.

268. Congressional Record, 68th Congress, 1st session, 11 February 1924, pp. 2242-2243.

Johnson expressed his lack of confidence in Secretary of Navy Edwin Denby. He felt this country "ought to sweep away every bribe giver, sweep away every bribe taker, sweep out of the Government every single individual who, innocently or ignorantly, has been a part of the filching of the public domain from the people of the United States." (Denby had allowed oil companies to lease federal lands and to drill for oil which, Johnson believed, should have been maintained as a strategic reserve).

269. Congressional Record, 68th Congress, 1st session, 26 February 1924, pp. 3142-3150.

Representative Harrison placed into the Record a number of newspaper clippings concerning Johnson's campaign for the presidency. He included the entire text of the speech Johnson delivered in Cleveland on January 3, 1924, in which Johnson laid out the major issues he would address, including the unfair selection process for delegates at the Republican Convention, tax reduction, the bonus bill for veterans, foreign policy, and the international court.

270. Congressional Record, 68th Congress, 1st session, 9 April 1924, pp. 5951-5952.

Johnson spoke on a bill to restrict the immigration of aliens into the United States. He said that in his lifetime he had observed Japanese farmers taking over the farmland near Sacramento and many residential blocks of that city now have a distinctly Japanese character. This happened at a time when the "gentleman's agreement" between the United States and Japan was supposed to be limiting the immigration of Japanese into America. Such a policy obviously was not working. On the other hand, the Chinese exclusion, because it was enacted by Congress, did limit Chinese immigration.

271. Congressional Record, 68th Congress, 1st session, 4 June 1924, pp. 10477-10480.

This was Johnson's first major Senate speech supporting the Boulder Canyon Dam--a bill he had introduced the previous December. Two "serious conditions" lent urgency to the bill: the annual floods of the Colorado River which destroyed life and property and the development of the Imperial Valley which demanded its own water supply and should no longer have to depend on a canal passing through Mexico. Private power companies opposed the development and were seeking a monopoly on the electricity produced at the dam. The power resources of the nation should not yield to private profit.

272. Congressional Record, 68th Congress, 2nd session, 16 December 1924, p. 643.

Johnson offered a constitutional amendment which would have allowed a plurality of electors in the electoral college, rather than a majority, to elect the president. Such an amendment would lessen the chances that an election would be determined by the House of Representatives. Although Johnson preferred a direct vote of the people for the president, he recognized that such a proposal was not feasible.

273. Congressional Record, 68th Congress, 2nd session, 19 December 1924, pp. 816-819.

Johnson supported Senator Norris's plan for government produced electric power at Muscle Shoals. The government had already spent $150 million on the project and Johnson argued that it should be completed and run by the government, not turned over to private corporations.

274. Congressional Record, 68th Congress, 2nd session, 27 January 1925, pp. 2507-2508.

Johnson spoke in favor of an increased wage for postal employees and against a bill which would have raised the revenue for the increase by increasing the postage rates paid by certain periodicals. Postal employees deserved a living wage.

275. Congressional Record, 68th Congress, 2nd session, 5 February 1925, pp. 2984-2993.

In a lengthy address, Johnson decried what had happened at an international conference in Paris on January 14, 1925. He expressed his view of the correct American policy: "letting America live her own life in her own way, unentangled by any political ties with Europe or any of Europe's nations." Such a position was not, he believed isolationist: "I would not be isolated from the rest of the world, of course, in any of those contacts which for 140 years we have always had." Applause from the galleries greeted the speech.

276. Congressional Record, 69th Congress, 1st session, 19 January 1926, pp. 2349-2355.

Johnson offered seven reasons why he opposed the World Court with or without reservations: (1) joining was a futile act; (2) ready means were already at hand to handle the same controversies; (3) joining the Court will "inevitably" take us into the League of Nations; (4) American questions should not be submitted to foreign judges; (5) America would be leaving behind a 140 year old policy; (6) joining the Court would involve us in European strife; (7) avoiding any question of consequence (because of reservations) would make us the "poltroon" among the nations of the earth.

277. Congressional Record, 69th Congress, 1st session, 21 April 1926, pp. 7891-7894.

Johnson spoke against a bill reducing the debt owed by Italy to the United States. It was not fair to the American people who had taken out Liberty loans. Foreign governments should not be treated better than American citizens. The New York bankers were behind the movement for reductions, but Johnson believed it was better to demand the full amount. Italy's ability to pay might improve: "Who can tell but the dream of empire of Mussolini may yet come true? . . . if his dream of empire should come true in 10, 15, or 20 years, Italy's capacity to pay might be infinitely greater."

278. Congressional Record, 69th Congress, 1st session, 17 June 1926, pp. 11427-11432.

Johnson spoke in favor of a bill to create a division of cooperative marketing in the Department of Agriculture and to encourage the formation of cooperatives throughout the country. In the Commerce clause of the Constitution, he found the government's right to act in the public interest.

279. Congressional Record, 69th Congress, 2nd session, 20 December 1926, pp. 759-761.

Answering a speech made by Vice President Dawes, Johnson spoke in favor of direct primaries. The people of the United States can be trusted to do the honest thing; political bosses will "never do that thing." Even allowing the voters to select all the delegates to a convention was not enough.

280. Congressional Record, 69th Congress, 2nd session, 3 January 1927, pp. 990-997.

Johnson argued the case for a strong Navy: "Today the Navy of the United States is in comparison with Great Britain and Japan, underbuilt, insufficient, inadequate, and so far inferior as to humiliate the national pride and imperil the national safety." America must rely on naval power and merchant marine power to defend herself militarily and economically. Since the Washington Conference of 1922, "Great Britain has laid down more than three times, Japan more than eleven times, France more than eight times, and Italy more than four times the number of ships which America has laid down. . ."

281.   Congressional Record, 69th Congress, 2nd session, 19 February 1927, pp. 4227-4231.

Speaking in favor of the Boulder Dam project, Johnson stressed that the project included flood control, reclamation, irrigation, and the end of dependence on Mexico for American water needs.   The dam would be 550 feet in height and store 26 million acre feet of water. Johnson tried to visualize for Easterners the impact that such a dam would have on the lives of the 60,000 inhabitants of the Imperial Valley.

282.   Congressional Record, 70th Congress, 1st session, 27 January 1928, pp. 2126-2130.

Speaking in favor of a bill to strengthen the merchant marine, Johnson stressed the importance of sea power: "There is nothing . . . that means more to the future of the Republic, to the prosperity of the people of this Nation, and generally to the perpetuity of our institutions than sea power."   Johnson also defended government activity in business as often the best means of handling a "national" problem. As American foreign trade had increased, American shipping had decreased.

283.   Congressional Record, 70th Congress, 1st session, 1 February 1928, pp. 2299-2307.

In a lengthy and dramatic speech, Johnson called for a congressional investigation of the coal mine strikes in progress in Ohio, West Virginia, and Pennsylvania.   Using newspaper reports and letters received from families and social workers involved, Johnson documented the terrible suffering the strikers were undergoing.   Johnson blamed the coal companies for refusing to bargain in good faith and for unilaterally repudiating a contract signed with the miners under government auspices in 1924.

284.   Congressional Record, 70th Congress, 1st session, 26 April 1928, pp. 7245-7253.

Johnson offered the history of the proposed Boulder Dam, explained the reasons for the measure, and described its various provisions section by section.   Johnson called the proposal "the greatest work of its character ever undertaken by legislation. . . ."   Furthermore, the undertaking would cost nothing: "Before . . . a single dollar [can be] expended, the United States Government must have in its hands wholly executed contracts which will repay every penny contemplated to be expended under the bill."

285.   Congressional Record, 70th Congress, 2nd session, 9 January 1929, p. 1409.

As a member of the special committee which investigated
alleged bribery actions of Senators Norris and Borah,
Johnson exonerated them.  He desired all senators to "pay
to them the full meed of admiration, respect, and love
which their constituencies have for them and which they
have so richly earned in a lifetime of devotion to the
public interest."

286.  Congressional Record, 70th Congress, 2nd session, 31
January 1929, pp. 2526-2535.

Johnson spoke in favor of a bill to build fifteen naval
cruisers.  They were needed to protect American commerce:
"Our exports are already over 20 percent greater than
those of any other one nation. . . ."  The disarmament
conference of 1922 had given naval superiority to Britain,
and the only way for the United States to obtain parity
was to initiate a building program.

287.  Congressional Record, 71st Congress, 1st session, 2
October 1929, pp. 4118-4123.

The Progressive party in 1912 had supported a non-partisan
tariff commission that would undertake scientific research
and report its findings to Congress.  Johnson, admittedly
a "protectionist," supported the same type of commission
in 1929.  He opposed flexible tariff provisions, but it
seemed that the Senate was going to support them.  Who
then would set the rates?  The Senate should never give up
its economic power to the president or to a presidential
agency.

288.  Congressional Record, 71st Congress, 1st session. 28
October 1929, pp. 4971-4972.

Johnson argued the need to protect the olive industries of
California and Arizona with a high tariff.  Labor costs in
the United States were much higher than they were in the
Mediterranean countries which exported olives to the U.S.

289.  Congressional Record, 70th Congress, 2nd session, 1
February 1930, p. 2835.

While offering an article to be included in the
Congressional Record, Johnson revealed his view of the Los
Angeles Times: "Any editorial utterance or any comment of
the Los Angeles Times is prima facie evidence of the
contrary. . . ."

290.  Congressional Record, 70th Congress, 2nd session, 22
April 1930, pp. 7416-7420.

Speaking in favor of strict regulation of immigration from
Mexico, Johnson stated, "Long ago it seemed to me
essential . . . that something should be done to curb, at

the earliest possible time, with the least possible harm, the immigration that is coming to us from Mexico."

291. Congressional Record, 70th Congress, 2nd session, 7 May 1930, pp. 8476-8478.

Johnson spoke against the nomination of John J. Parker to the Supreme Court. Johnson found that Parker's background did not commend him as a judge, that his appointment was purely political in character, and that previous lower court decisions by Parker had shown him on the wrong side of the "fundamental economic questions concerning which the line of cleavage has been so sharply drawn in our country." Comparing himself to Abraham Lincoln in objecting to the Dred Scott decision, Johnson took issue with Parker's decision in the "Red Jacket" case (allowing "yellow dog" contracts).

292. Congressional Record, 71st Congress, 2nd session, 19 June 1930, pp. 11187-11190. (Radio address of 18 June 1930).

Senator Moses placed into the Record a speech Johnson delivered over the CBS radio network about the London Naval Treaty. "As an American" Johnson opposed the treaty. The Washington Naval Conference of 1922 showed how easily fixed ratios of warships could be circumvented. The treaty would result in no savings to taxpayers and the "great preponderance of testimony" was against the treaty. The treaty "does not measure up to our material necessities and it falls far short of our ideals."

293. Congressional Record, 71st Congress, Special session, 11 July 1930, pp. 112-115.

Johnson opposed the London Naval Treaty because it failed to follow the ship ratios fixed in Washington in 1922 and provided for readjustments in 1935. American heavy cruisers seemed to be limited without commensurate limitations on British and Japanese ships. Britain gained more from the treaty than did the United States.

294. Congressional Record, 71st Congress, Special session, 17 July 1930, p. 209.

When threatened with a cloture vote to allow the Senate to vote on the London Naval Treaty, Johnson responded: "Go on with your majority; put on your cloture if you wish to put it on. The only times in reality, save possibly once, that cloture has been put on this body has been when we were acting in behalf of some foreign adventure or misadventure."

295. Congressional Record, 71st Congress, Special session, 17 July 1930, pp.222-230.

Johnson spoke of the difficulties faced by members of the opposition to the London Naval Treaty.    "Reduction of armament" had become an irresistible slogan.    The Washington conference of 1922 had not brought the predicted reduction in armaments and the 1930 conference would not do what its supporters predicted.    America needed sea power to keep the "open door" policy in China and to protect the Philippines.

296.  Congressional Record, 71st Congress, 3rd session, 5 January 1931, pp. 1369-1371.  (Radio address of 20 December 1930).

Senator McNary placed into the Record Johnson's radio address against United States adherence to the World Court.    Those who attempted unsuccessfully to get the United States into the League of Nations directly were now attempting to do it "indirectly and surreptitiously" by advocating that we join the World Court.    Joining the court "would not contribute to world peace or a better understanding among the nations of the world."

297.  Congressional Record, 72nd Congress, 1st session, 15 December 1931, pp. 539-540.

Johnson opposed any moratorium on debts owed to the United States by foreign countries.    Extensions of time should be allowed generously, but the United States should stand behind its rights to repayment.    To do otherwise was to subordinate the rights of the people of the United States to those of international bankers who were being repaid.

298.  Congressional Record, 72nd Congress, 1st session, 12 February 1932, pp. 3810-3813.

The Reconstruction Corporation had aided the banks and the railroads; the Farm Board Act was supposed to aid the farmers; now, Johnson argued, was the time to help the man at the bottom and he spoke in favor of a relief measure proposed by Senator La Follette.    Testimony had revealed high unemployment, malnourishment, and tuberculosis among children.

299.  Congressional Record, 72nd Congress, 1st session, 15 March 1932, pp. 6052-6062.

Without a Senate staff, but with the aid of several "younger members" of the press, Johnson investigated the foreign debt question.    International bankers had "unloaded" bonds on a gullible American public.    Now the bonds were worth half or less of what had been invested.    Banks had bribed foreign officials for the right to handle their country's loans.    The federal government had a responsibility to its investing citizens.

300. Congressional Record, 72nd Congress, 1st session, 30
March 1932, pp. 7119-7121. (Address of 27 October 1931).

Senator McNary placed into the Record Johnson's speech on
naval preparedness.   Delivered on Theodore Roosevelt's
birthday, Johnson quoted Roosevelt's admonition that
preparation was the best way to avoid war.   Since 1922 the
United States had gone from a position of naval
superiority to one of inferiority and still there was talk
of a "naval holiday."   The primary purpose of a navy is
protection, not aggression.

301. Congressional Record, 72nd Congress, 1st session, 16
May 1932, pp. 10285-10288.

Johnson used bitter sarcasm to denounce those who would
support a 10 percent tax on 10 cent movie admissions, but
seemingly did little to tax those with million dollar
incomes.   As he often did, Johnson referred to the $250
million moratorium on war debts which the Senate had
approved earlier: "Every dollar given Europe is now being
paid by American taxpayers."

302. Congressional Record, 72nd Congress, 1st session, 2
June 1932, pp. 11817-11818.

Johnson spoke against the across the board 10 percent
reduction in federal salaries.   It was not fair to the man
who made the least.   It took from him "in part food and
clothing. . . . in part shelter and light. . . . in part
the right to bring up his children as American children
are entitled to be brought up."   Those who were unable to
protect themselves needed "the protecting arm of those who
represent them upon this floor."

303. Congressional Record, 72nd Congress, 1st session, 9
July 1932, pp. 14953-14955.

Johnson felt that the most important thing Congress could
do was to pass a relief bill.   With the House and
president at odds over whether loans should be made to
private corporations or to individuals, no bill seemed to
be possible.   Johnson blamed Hoover: "If any man is
responsible to the American people for the lack of relief
to human beings in this land, it is just one man, one man
alone. . . ."

304. Congressional Record, 72nd Congress, 2nd session, 25
January 1933, pp. 2474-2477.

Johnson objected to any international conference at which
foreign countries would attempt to induce the United
States to reduce the debt owed.   Johnson quoted British
spokesmen who expressed such a desire.   While people in
America were going hungry, the government should not be

forgiving justly owed debts.

305. Congressional Record, 72nd Congress, 2nd session, 2 February 1933, pp. 3175-3176.

Johnson spoke at the behest of the American manufacturers who bid on equipment for the Boulder Dam project but lost to lower bids by European companies. Johnson felt projects sponsored by the government should be completed by American firms.

306. Congressional Record, 73rd Congress, 1st session, 28 April 1933, p. 2541.

Johnson paid tribute to President Franklin Roosevelt, "the fine and gallant gentleman who sits in the White House today and who, with a courage that is inspiriting and inspiring, sits there ready to do whatever lies in his power."

307. Congressional Record, 73rd Congress, 1st session, 31 May 1933, pp. 4651-4655.

Speaking out for disabled war veterans, Johnson sought to exempt them from any cuts in their disability payments: "I do not want to go back to my home and see the legless man, the man without sight in his eyes, compelled to become an object of charity upon my city or upon my friends."

308. Congressional Record, 73rd Congress, 1st session, 6 June 1933, pp. 5085-5089.

Johnson fought to exempt publicly owned electric companies from federal taxation. Exempting government activities from taxation was not a new idea. The Senate should not yield to the arguments of privately owned companies that contended that such action was discriminatory and unjust. The not-for-profit company returned its "profits" to the people and thus paid its "taxes."

309. Congressional Record, 73rd Congress, 2nd session, 5 February 1934, pp. 1915-1920.

Johnson spoke in favor of legislation which prohibited federal district courts from suspending orders of state regulatory agencies while the case was still being tried in the state courts. Nothing prevented a utility company from pursuing a favorable ruling in a state and federal court simultaneously and dismissing any case where it appeared to be losing, but continuing in that arena where it seemed to have a better chance. What Johnson called "two bites of the cherry" was not available to the ordinary citizen and Johnson argued it should not be available to utility companies.

310.  Congressional Record, 73rd Congress, 2nd session, 7 May 1934, pp. 8191-8194.

Johnson warned the Senate that a debt payment by Great Britain was due the following month and that should the payment not be made in full, Great Britain would be considered in default.  According to the Johnson Act, no nation in default could sell foreign bonds or securities in the United States.  Previously, the president had accepted a token payment by Great Britain and had declared the nation was not in default, but such a ruling was no longer possible under the new legislation.

311.  Congressional Record, 73rd Congress, 2nd session, 12 May 1934, pp. 8722-8723.

Johnson attempted to expand the authorization of the Reconstruction Finance Corporation to allow loans to be made to public utilities.  The public power agency in Los Angeles needed funds to buy out the competing private utility in the area and to contract with the Boulder Dam Corporation to purchase power when that project was completed.

312.  Congressional Record, 73rd Congress, 2nd session, 30 May 1934, pp. 9959-9964.

Johnson argued as he did in 1922 and again in 1929 against a flexible tariff.  It was the Senate's duty to decide rates and this obligation should not be given to the executive branch.  Johnson claimed he was holding the "Democratic" position on the issue, and that Democrats should join him in upholding what was their traditional position.

313.  Congressional Record, 74th Congress, 1st session, 16 January 1935, pp. 479-490.

In Johnson's first major speech against the United States joining the World Court, he quoted his favorite saying of Lincoln's that "I am not bound to win, but I am bound to be true.  I am not bound to succeed, but I am bound to live up to what light I have. . ."  Johnson claimed the only reason offered for joining the court was "to meddle and muddle."  He added: "To say that our entry into this Court will bring peace to the world is to me the most silly thing that ever was advanced by sensible human beings."  The United States had relied on arbitration of disputes for over 100 years, and Johnson argued that such treaties held more promise than any court.

314.  Congressional Record, 74th Congress, 1st session, 28 January 1935, pp. 1039-1043.

As the debate on the World Court came to a close, Johnson

once again offered his reasons for its rejection.    To
Johnson it came down to a single question: "Shall we go
into foreign politics?"    Johnson, of course, said "no" and
reminded his listeners of the views of Washington, Adams,
Jackson, Cleveland, McKinley and others who opposed
entanglement with Europe.

315. Congressional Record, 74th Congress, 1st session, 15
May 1935, pp. 3706-3707.

Johnson favored the McCarren amendment which would have
obligated the federal government to pay wage rates no less
than the prevailing wage to anyone employed on federal
relief projects.    Johnson argued that the federal
government had followed such a policy in regard to public
buildings and to the Tennessee Valley Authority, and that
more than 20 states had statutes requiring such payment.

316. Congressional Record, 74th Congress, 1st session, 20
June 1935, pp. 9756-9762.

Johnson was placed in an awkward position by the case of
Rush D. Holt who was elected by the people of West
Virginia to represent them in the Senate even though he
was not the required 30 years old.    Holt presented himself
six months later (having reached the required age) and the
Senate had to decide whether to seat him or not.    The
popular will was clear to Johnson but so was the
Constitution which Johnson felt disqualified Holt. Johnson
reluctantly voted against Holt based on precedents set by
the Senate in the cases of Albert Gallatin and James
Shields, but Holt was seated.

317. Congressional Record, 74th Congress, 1st session, 24
July 1935, pp. 11770-11771.

Johnson spoke in favor of reducing an appropriation for a
building for the General Accounting Office from    $11.15
million to $4.7 million.    In addition to the economy
issue, Johnson spoke against an unregulated right of
eminent domain.    Federal law allowed the government to act
in ways the state government could not and Johnson felt
federal regulations treated property owners in the
District of Columbia unfairly.

318. Congressional Record, 74th Congress, 1st session, 24
August 1935, pp. 14430-14432.

Johnson favored a joint resolution which prohibited the
export of arms and ammunition to any belligerent nation
and restricted travel by American citizens on belligerent
ships during the war.    He warned, however, that such a
resolution would not end forever the chances of America
becoming involved in a war.    He also warned that such a
policy claiming to be "neutral" was not in fact neutral if

one side could manufacture its own arms and the other could not.

319. <u>Congressional Record</u>, 75th Congress, 1st session, 3 March 1937, pp. 1778-1784.

Johnson opposed an amendment to the Neutrality Act which allowed the president, at his discretion, to prohibit the use of American vessels to carry certain goods to belligerent nations.  Such a bill made the United States the ally of Great Britain in the Atlantic and of Japan in the Pacific since they controlled shipping in those areas and only their ships would be able to carry the restricted goods.  The "cash and carry" principle favored the nations with the best navies, not necessarily those with the best cause.

320. <u>Congressional Record</u>, 75th Congress, 1st session, 1 April 1937, pp. 3021-3022.

Johnson spoke out strongly against the use of the "sit-down" strike.  "As a friend of union labor," Johnson would use federal troops, if necessary, to clear an area held by such tactics.

321. <u>Congressional Record</u>, 75th Congress, 1st session, 22 July 1937, p. 7381.

Johnson's exclamation, "Glory be to God!" was greeted by applause and provided a fitting conclusion to the debate to reorganize the Supreme Court.  Roosevelt's proposal was referred back to the Committee on the Judiciary and never heard of again.

322. <u>Congressional Record</u>, 75th Congress, 1st session, 17 August 1937, pp. 9101-9102.

Johnson opposed the nomination of Hugo L. Black of Alabama to the Supreme Court.  Johnson argued that Black was ineligible because he voted for the Supreme Court's retirement act (thus voting to increase the emoluments to that office).  He declared that Black had neither the temperament nor disposition to fill a judicial position.

323. <u>Congressional Record</u>, 75th Congress, 3rd session, 1 February 1938, pp. 1326-1327.

Johnson reacted to President Roosevelt's speech in which he argued that aggressive countries ought to be "quarantined."  He wondered what was the foreign policy of the United States: would FDR follow through on his threat or not?  Johnson insisted that once such a statement was made, the president had to back it up or admit a mistake.

324. <u>Congressional Record</u>, 75th Congress, 3rd session, 14

February 1938, pp. 1871-1873.

Johnson argued against giving Secretary of Agriculture Wallace the power to set acreage limitations on various crops.   He quoted earlier statements made by Wallace to show that he did not favor giving government officials the type of power the proposed bill would give to him. Johnson feared the agriculture bill "will be the beginning of regimentation of industry in this country."

325.   Congressional Record, 75th Congress, 3rd session, 16 March 1938, pp. 3461-3465.

Johnson reacted strongly against a proposed reorganization of government agencies which included the abolition of the Comptroller General's Office.   An officer of the executive department would replace an officer of Congress, a "further transference of power to the President of the United States at the expense of Congress."

326.   Congressional Record, 75th Congress, 3rd session, 18 March 1938, p. 3644.

Johnson spoke in a very emotional tone in favor of an amendment to the reoganization of government bill which would have subjected any proposed changes to House and Senate approval before they became law.   Still recovering from serious illness, Johnson said, "I am not going to serve here, perhaps, very long," but "let us stand here as sentient human beings, as men who desire to do the right, as men who do not fear power wherever it exists. . . ."

327.   Congressional Record, 76th Congress, 1st session, 23 January 1939, pp. 619-621.

Johnson spoke against the nomination of Harry Hopkins as secretary of commerce.   The selection of cabinet members was not "a personal matter of the President," but a matter for the Senate to accept or reject.   Johnson pointed out those senators who had voted against the nomination of Charles Warren as attorney general thirteen years earlier to show that the Senate took its responsibilities seriously.

328.   Congressional Record, 76th Congress, 1st session, 1 February 1939, pp. 1015-1016.

Johnson sharply criticized the administration for not telling the American public that French agents were in the United States attempting to purchase military aircraft. If a French pilot, testing one of the planes, had not crashed, the American public would not have been aware such purchases were being made.   Such sales took America "to the brink of war" and they should not be made in secret.

329. <u>Congressional</u> <u>Record</u>, 76th Congress, 1st session, 2 March 1939, pp. 2131-2139. See also <u>Vital</u> <u>Speeches</u>, 5 (March 1939), 348-352.

Johnson showed the changing nature of American foreign policy by comparing statements made by FDR in 1935 and 1936 (which seemed to support nonalignment with any nation) with more recent statements beginning with the "quarantine" speech of 1937 and continuing to the present.

330. <u>Congressional</u> <u>Record</u>, 76th Congress, 1st session, 24 July 1939, pp. 9838-9840.

Johnson spoke against a new treaty with Panama which he claimed would undermine the ability of the United States to protect the Panama Canal. Joint decisions would replace unilateral U.S. decisions, taking time and, perhaps, preventing needed actions. The Panamanians had been treated fairly under previous treaties and there was no reason to change the present relationship.

331. <u>Congressional</u> <u>Record</u>, 76th Congress, 2nd session, 20 October 1939, pp. 628-632.

In one of his longest and most emotional efforts in some time, Johnson argued against the repeal of the arms embargo. Such a move would end American neutrality and gradually lead the United States to war against Germany. Johnson saw a number of similarities between the present situation and the circumstances which eventually involved the United States in World War I. The first war had not had the desired effect against tyranny and a second war would not be any better.

332. <u>Congressional</u> <u>Record</u> <u>Appendix</u>, 76th Congress, 2nd session, 27 October 1939, pp. 561-563. (Radio Address of 24 October 1939).

Senator Gerald Nye placed Johnson's speech against revision of the arms embargo into the <u>Record</u>. Speaking on the NBC radio network, Johnson warned that any change would end the neutrality of the United States and aid the Allies. Taking the side of Britain and France would surely involve the United States in the war against Germany, a war which must be avoided.

333. <u>Congressional</u> <u>Record</u> <u>Appendix</u>, 76th Congress, 3rd session, 21 October 1940, pp. 6472-6474. (Radio Address of 18 October 1940). See also <u>Vital</u> <u>Speeches</u>, 7 (November 1940), 52-55.

Johnson spoke over the CBS Radio network against a third term for Franklin Roosevelt. He called the issue of a third term of more importance to Americans than any issue, including the war in Europe. Democrats had respected the two term tradition from their founding, but now an ambitious man was attempting to do what Washington and Jefferson warned should not be done. Willkie and McNary faced "almost insuperable odds" and Johnson did not support them on every issue, but on the most important question they were right.

334. Congressional Record Appendix, 77th Congress, 1st session, 25 February 1941, pp. A826-A828. (Radio Address of 24 February 1941).

Senator Nye had Johnson's National Radio Forum address on modifications of the Lend-Lease Act placed into the Appendix. The proposal gave too much power to the president. He could decide which nation was an aggressor and what should be done about it. America was not in danger of invasion. The same propaganda that had gotten the United States involved in the World War I was being heard again. Johnson's band in the Senate was "small but determined, and will fight to the end."

335. Congressional Record, 77th Congress, 1st session, 7 March 1941, pp. 1961-1962.

Johnson attempted to amend a defense appropriation measure by adding that no funds could be used to support American troops outside the Western Hemisphere in time of war. He argued that both political parties had promised in the 1940 campaign that American "lads" would not fight in Europe and he challenged his colleagues to put their promises into action. His speech was met by applause, but the amendment failed.

336. Congressional Record Appendix, 77th Congress, 1st session, 2 June 1941, pp. A2594-A2596. (Radio Address of 31 May 1941). See also Vital Speeches, 7 (June 1941), 514-517.

Senator Shipstead had Johnson's address delivered over the NBC radio network printed in the Appendix. Johnson spoke under the auspices of the America First Committee. To this point, the president had always asked for aid "short of war" to help Britain against Germany, but now "that phrase was being omitted. We are doing everything we can to help Britain and still it isn't enough." The United States was not prepared for war, but it was slowly being dragged in.

337. Congressional Record, 77th Congress, 1st session, 28 July 1941, pp. 6335-6336.

Johnson spoke in defense of Burton K. Wheeler when Wheeler was accused of near treason by Secretary of War Stimson for distributing cards to members of the armed forces asking them to write to the president and to tell him that they were opposed to American entry in the European war.

To "manifestations of applause in the galleries," Johnson cried: "Never mind how many are with you; stand up; there will be one at least with you in the fight."

338. Congressional Record, 77th Congress, 1st session, 7 August 1941, pp. 6847-6850.

Johnson spoke against an extension of the time men drafted by the selective service system would have to serve. He argued that the Senate had promised to limit their service to 12 months and that the Senate should keep its promise. Johnson summed up his attitude toward both Hitler and Stalin: "I would securely lock them in an elevated cage and let them fight it out." During Johnson's speech the gallery was admonished for applauding his effort.

339. Congressional Record Appendix, 77th Congress, 1st session, 7 November 1941, pp. A5040-A5042. (Radio Address of 6 November 1941). See also Vital Speeches, 8 (December 1941), 120-124.

Senator La Follette had Johnson's address on the NBC radio network printed in the Appendix. Almost one-half of the speech consisted of excerpts from remarks of President Roosevelt which proclaimed the advantages of neutrality. With them Johnson heartily agreed. But "by deceit and subterfuge" we are on the brink of war. The president and his cabinet want us to "fight another country's war."

340. Congressional Record, 77th Congress, 1st session, 7 November 1941, pp. 8670-8671.

Johnson spoke against the arming of merchant ships. It would inevitably lead to war. Often referring to his age (75), Johnson said he did "not want upon my soul the infamy of taking this country into war when I believe fully it ought not be taken into war."

341. Congressional Record, 77th Congress, 2nd session, 17 February 1942, pp. 1332-1333.

Johnson called for increased defense measures on the West Coast: "Without such consideration, we are likely to see in the near future another Pearl Harbor; without it we are likely to see despoiled the land which we regard with such a degree of pleasure."

342. Congressional Record, 77th Congress, 2nd session, 23 October 1942, pp. 8566-8570.

Johnson spoke against a measure to lower the draft age to 18. Even in England they did not send boys out of the country until they were 19 1/2. In New Zealand, boys were not sent overseas until they were 21. Johnson realized that his position was hopeless, but he felt: "a Senator has a right to come upon this floor and say a word in behalf of children."

343.  Congressional Record, 77th Congress, 2nd session, 4 December 1942, pp. 9320-9322.

Johnson argued that a joint resolution dealing with American obligations in Panama should be treated as a treaty rather than as normal legislation and thus required a two-thirds approval for passage.  The legislation amended treaties of 1903 and 1936.  The Senate should jealously guard its right to ratify treaties against those who have made "a determined effort for some years to take that right away."

344.  Congressional Record, 78th Congress, 1st session, 5 November 1943, pp. 9210-9211.

Still recovering from serious illness "with but half my voice and half my hearing," Johnson explained why he was unable to participate in the debate over the Connally resolution, pledging post-war international collaboration. His doctors and his wife forbade his injecting himself into the debate "for fear I should retard the recovery." He could only exhort his colleagues and all Americans "to be just Americans," and ended with "God bless America."

345.  Congressional Record, 78th Congress, 2nd session, 5 September 1944, pp. 7510-7511.

Upon the death of former Senator George W. Norris of Nebraska, Johnson repeated a tribute to Norris he had first spoken on December 19, 1924, when Norris was attempting to have the Muscle Shoals Project (Tennessee Valley Authority) completed.  Norris had been called by an opponent a "dreamer" and Johnson defended the dreamers of history.  To Norris he said, "Your dreams, sir, mean that humanity may benefit, people may prosper, and human beings may be a bit happier."

346.  Congressional Record, 79th Congress, 1st session, 17 April 1945, pp. 3418-3420.

Fearful that a proposed treaty with Mexico would take away water from those living in the Imperial Valley of California, Johnson made his last important speech in the Senate.  He praised those men who ventured into the desert, built homes, and grew vegetables for their fellow citizens.  He begged the Senate "to give them a square deal, rather than to reach over into Mexico and give Mexico a square deal."

# Appendix

## Manuscript Collections

Most of Johnson's unpublished correspondence can be found in the Johnson Papers (1), but some letters are available in the following manuscript collections:

| Collection | Location | Union Catelog of Manuscripts Number |
|---|---|---|
| Beveridge, Albert J. | Manuscript Division, Library of Congress | MS 62-2706 |
| Bloch, Claude C. | Manuscript Division, Library of Congress | MS 71-1336 |
| Borah, William E. | Manuscript Division, Library of Congress | MS 78-1690 |
| Borchard, Edwin M. | Yale University Library | MS 77-2104 |
| Cooke, Morris L. | FDR Library (Hyde Park) | MS 65-29 |
| Cutting, Bronson | Manuscript Division, Library of Congress | MS 62-4632 |
| Dickson, Edward A. | University of California, Los Angeles | MS 71-845 |
| Garfield, James R. | Manuscript Division, Library of Congress | MS 59-262 |
| Glasscock, William E. | West Virginia University Library | MS 59-160 |
| Haines, Lynn | Minnesota Historical Society | MS 60-1374 |
| Haynes, John R. | University of California, Los Angeles | MS 62-122 |
| Hichborn, Franklin | University of California, Los Angeles | MS 62-533 |
| Ickes, Harold L. | Manuscript Division, Library of Congress | MS 60-145 |
| Johnson, Hiram W. | University of Oregon Library | MS 66-1298 |

| Collection | Location | Union Catelog of Manuscripts Number |
|---|---|---|
| Jones, Herbert C. | Stanford University Library | MS 65-2010 |
| Kent, William | Yale University Library | MS 62-3510 |
| Knox, Dudley W. | Manuscript Division, Library of Congress | MS 71-1371 |
| La Follette Family | Manuscript Division, Library of Congress | MS 82-1203 |
| Lissner, Meyer | Stanford University Library | MS 65-860 |
| Marx, Guido H. | Stanford University Library | MS 67-2074 |
| McCamant, Wallace | University of Oregon Library | MS 62-2111 |
| McKinley, William B. | Syracuse University Library | MS 70-713 |
| McNary, Charles L. | Manuscript Division, Library of Congress | MS 60-1414 |
| Moore, John B. | Manuscript Division, Library of Congress | MS 61-3281 |
| Neumiller, Charles L. | Holt-Atherton Center, Univ. of the Pacific | MS 82-2015 |
| Norbeck, Peter | University of Missouri Library | MS 60-3127 |
| Norris, George W. | Manuscript Division, Library of Congress | MS 62-2698 |
| Rowell, Chester H. | Bancroft Library, Univ. of CA, Berkeley | MS 71-789 |
| Smith, Joseph E. | University of Washington Library | MS 64-1271 |
| Teigan, Henry G. | Minnesota Historical Society | MS 60-260 |
| Vandenberg, Arthur H. | Bentley Library, Univ. of Michigan | MS 80-1680 |
| Van Valkenburg, Edwin | Houghton Library, Harvard University | MS 65-1304 |
| Walker, Guy M. | DePauw University Library | MS 68-892 |
| Washburn, Stanley | Manuscript Division, Library of Congress | MS 60-146 |

# Index

## About the Authors

MICHAEL A. WEATHERSON is an Assistant Professor in the Department of Speech Communication at Southeast Missouri State University.

HAL BOCHIN is Professor of Speech Communication at California State University, Fresno. He has contributed essays and articles to *American Orators Before 1900* (Greenwood Press, 1987), *In Search of Justice, Communication*, and *Communication Education*. He has also prepared three debate handbooks: *Law Enforcement: Issues and Evidence, Guaranteeing Product Safety: Issues and Evidence*, and *Controlling Land Use: Issues and Evidence*.